Eat
Like a
Local

SHANGHAI

BLOOMSBURY PUBLISHING
LONDON • OXFORD • NEW YORK • NEW DELHI • SYDNEY

Welcome to Shanghai

Shanghai is an outward-looking city that has built its fortunes on trade… and spent them on food. The name of the city, 上海, literally translates as 'on the sea' and it is now the largest shipping port in the world, drawing influences and talent from far and wide that continue to shape its culinary landscape today.

For the visitor, there are many advantages to eating and drinking in the world's most populous city. With enough restaurants and bars to cater to the 24 million residents – both well-known venues and hidden gems – there is no chance that you will go hungry. However, navigating the city's sheer size, the breakneck speed of its redevelopment and the often hilariously mistranslated menus can test even the most seasoned traveller. This guide aims to help you sail through all those murky waters.

The city has one foot rooted in tradition and the other sprinting towards modernisation, so the Shanghainese are spoiled for choice: hipster independent coffee shops or gimmicky 'cheese tea' cafés sit comfortably alongside the astonishingly diverse classic Chinese cuisine.

The Shanghainese are pioneers of tech innovation, too. There's an app that summons a chef to come to your home to make dinner, fetch a barman to make cocktails, or simply to order a takeaway. China aims to be the first cashless society and Shanghai is driving that change.

The city has some of the greatest dining experiences in the world, from those as simple (though sublime) as a bowl of hand-pulled noodles formed before your eyes, to cutting-edge restaurants that use augmented reality to bring the table to life. Meanwhile, Shanghai-style home cooking is renowned both for its seafood and fresh seasonal produce and for incorporating artisanal delicacies from neighbouring provinces, such as Jinhua ham and Shaoxing wine.

All that you need is time to explore the city's secrets and appreciate its diverse flavours. And, of course, this guide.

Explore the City

The Huangpu river splits Shanghai in two: older Puxi (浦西) and newer Pudong (浦东). (Xi 西 = West, Dong 东 = East.)

Xuhui (徐汇) (The Former French Concession)

Western expat central, with tree-lined boulevards and independent coffee shops. Both Wulumuqi Lu (乌鲁木齐路) and Anfu Lu (安福路) are long and charming roads with mixes of old and new Shanghai. Stroll down Hengshan Lu (衡山路) to Xujiahui (徐家汇), surrounded by malls and chain restaurants. To the west is Jiao Tong University (交通大学) with nearby LGBT clubs and bars. Modern boundaries slice up the old Concession; most is in Xuhui; parts spill over into Jing'an and Huangpu.

Jing'an (静安)

A huge gold facsimile of the Jing'an Temple (静安寺) is surrounded by luxury malls here. The district is a hectic mix of contemporary Chinese construction and some of the finest Art Deco architecture in the world.

Huangpu (黄浦)

Nowhere is more iconic than The Bund (外滩). Colonial-era banks, hotels and Michelin-starred restaurants line the river. The evening light show starts every day at 7pm and ends at 11pm sharp. Nanjing Lu (南京路) begins here, cutting west through the city with world-famous fashion brands on each side of the road. Tourist hotspots of Yu Garden (豫园), Xintiandi (新天地) and Tianzifang (田子方) have been renovated, while the Old City is being gentrified.

Pudong (浦东)

Pudong is larger than the whole of New York City, although sparsely populated by comparison. Lujiazui (陆家嘴) has some of the tallest buildings in the world, with rooftop bars and luxury hotel restaurants aplenty. Xinchang Water Town has avoided the tourist trap and is scattered with handicraft basket and tinker shops. Disneyland and the adjacent resort are home to several American chain restaurants.

Changning (长宁)

Gubei (古北) is Asian expat hub here, filled with Japanese, Korean and Thai restaurants. Columbia Circle (上生新所) has stylish eateries inside a charming Art Deco country club, while family-friendly Zhongshan Park (中山公园) is one of the few spots in Shanghai where you can picnic.

Putuo (普陀)

Home to the majority of the city's Muslim population. The district is filled with artists, open studios and trendy coffee shops.

Hongkou (虹口)

Historically the Jewish ghetto; sadly none of the food heritage survives.

Minhang (闵行)

This crosses the river. Qibao Water Town (七宝) is easy to reach by metro.

Outer Districts

Songjiang (松江) has the Chinese answer to every Chinatown: Thames Town (泰晤士小镇), a replica of parts of London, with a smattering of Oxford. The bars even serve specially brewed beer. Qingpu (青浦) is the city's most easterly district; take the metro to Zhujiajiao Water Town (朱家角) for an eclectic mix of old Shanghainese cuisine and delicious food gifts. Chongming (崇明) is an island district off the north-east coast of Shanghai, almost entirely agricultural; during the summer months, you can hire bicycles, explore a national park or visit a biodynamic farm.

Meet the Locals

Michael Zee

@symmetrybreakfast

Michael is creator of Instagram account @symmetrybreakfast, a best-selling cookbook author, a tea connoisseur... and a little bit Chinese, as his grandfather is a native Shanghai ren (上海人). When he is not making and photographing breakfast, Michael works as a consultant introducing Western food brands to the Chinese market, and writes about Chinese food. He lives in Shanghai with husband Mark and Kebab their cat.

Jamie Barys

untourfoodtours.com

Jamie, from Tennessee, has lived in China since 2007. Whether she's exploring Shanghai's hidden hole-in-the-wall restaurants or sneaking into kitchens to snag recipes, she's always hungry. Jamie is Chief Eating Officer of UnTour Food Tours, China's top culinary tour company.

Wei Diao

ohashanghai.com

Co-founder of architecture studio OHA Shanghai and owner of Bar No. 3, OHA café-eatery and Blackbird. Wei explores new dining experiences, finding ways to rethink conventional culinary formats.

Jenny Gao

flybyjing.com

Jenny is the founder of Fly By Jing, a line of all-natural, artisanal food products celebrating the vibrant street food culture of Sichuan. She has explored Chinese food as a writer, cook and restaurateur for 10 years and featured in *New York Magazine*, the *Travel Channel*, the *BBC* and *Vice*.

Camden Hauge

@camdenhauge

Born in America, Camden worked her way from London to Shanghai in the world of advertising, not-so-secretly nurturing a passion for food and drink. In 2015 she opened Egg, then Bitter and Bird in 2018. She is the driving force behind events agency Social Supply, which runs Shanghai Supperclub, Cocktail Cinema, Liveroom and Feast food festival.

Xiaoyi Liu

restauranthunter.net

Born and bred in Shanghai, food blogger, PR and marketing consultant Xiaoyi worked in NYC for five years before moving back to Shanghai. She started Restaurant Hunter (觅食) food and travel blog four years ago. She contributes to *Elle*, *Condé Nast Traveler* and the *Michelin Guide Shanghai*.

Cat Nelson

@_catnelson

Former editor-in-chief of *Time Out Shanghai*, Cat moved to China nearly a decade ago, to research rural development and sustainable agriculture, before starting to write about food and travel. When not eating or drinking Aperol spritzes, you can find her dancing to Italian disco or napping.

Betty Richardson

bettyrichardson.com

Food writer, food stylist and photographer Betty is a former food and restaurant critic for local magazine *That's Shanghai*. She is a voracious lover of Chinese food in all its forms, with a particular interest in Jiangnan and Cantonese cuisines. She also took the photos for this book.

Alex Xu

@a_____xu

A former cook and restaurateur from Shanghai, wine-grower Alex has worked on estates in New Zealand, Australia and at Domaine Dujac in Burgundy. He now grows Pinot Noir and Chardonnay at the foot of the Jade Dragon Snow Mountain, aiming to grow grapes for pure, balanced and delicious wines that reflect the beauty of their surroundings.

DJ Zhang

@shanghaigirleats

Taking advantage of her Chinese metabolism, DJ started the blog Shanghai Girl Eats in 2013, as a way of telling her future boyfriend what restaurants to take her to for dinner. And she isn't even joking. When not stuffing her face with Shanghai's various dumpling delights, she can be found gorging on foie gras somewhere on the Bund. She has been described by close friends as 'salty as a bottle of soy sauce'.

A note on mobile payment in Shanghai

Sometime soon, China will become the world's first cashless society. Mega apps like WeChat and Alipay have replaced the need to carry a physical wallet and are absolutely indispensible to the lives of locals in Shanghai. At street food stalls, coffee shops, convenience shops and restaurants, you'll see a green QR code for WeChat, or a blue one for Alipay. Payment is a simple matter of scanning the code with the app and transferring the amount on the bill. Unfortunately, Alipay is only available to those with a Chinese bank account, but WeChat can be set up with a foreign card, some patience and some technical knowhow.

All venues in this guide take cash, but not all take international cards; almost none take American Express. It's not uncommon to visit a coffee shop that only takes WeChat pay and will refuse even exact change.

BREAKFAST & BRUNCH

Few cities in the world offer so much choice at breakfast. On most Shanghai streets you find early-morning vendors selling *baozi* (包子), steamed buns filled with pork or vegetables; a lady with a blender making fresh hot soy milk (*dou jiang* 豆浆); or a team rolling, stretching and frying *youtiao* (油条), deep-fried dough sticks that find their way into many other breakfast items.

The city's famous *xiaolongbao* dumplings (小笼包) are eaten the world over, but their lesser-known cousins *shengjianbao* (生煎包) are really the star of the show at breakfast. Their skins are thicker than other *bao*, while all appreciate their gloriously fried bottoms.

Jianbing (煎饼) is perhaps Shanghai's (and China's) most popular and widely available breakfast, though it originates in Tianjin. Don't be put off by a long queue; the cooks make these faster than you can eat, so you won't be waiting long. *Jianbing* is a thin crêpe, topped with a cracked egg, then smeared with a sweet brown sauce and sprinkled with pickles, coriander, Chinese chives, pepper, a cracker and maybe some chilli sauce. Using what looks like a paint scraper, at lightning speed, the whole thing is removed from the hot plate, folded, cut in half and thrown into a bag. You will most certainly want to document the process.

At weekends, the Shanghainese are just as big fans of brunch as anyone else. Restaurants such as Highline (see page 16) serve international favourites – chicken and waffles or eggs Benedict – with a side of iconic skyline and bottomless cocktails and (unsurprisingly) often need booking ahead.

For breakfast, see also Lao Di Fang and Pain Chaud (pages 32 and 45). For brunch, see also Cha's, RAC, The Cannery, PHÉNIX at the PuLi and Seventh Son (pages 49, 85, 81, 90 and 91).

① Egg

Recommended by Michael Zee

"Egg is the very antithesis of hype. It has a solid, seasonal and constantly evolving menu of inventive dishes for all times of day. A perfect spot if you want somewhere quiet to sit and work with a delicious home-made cake and a coffee. Also keep an eye out for the schedule of supper clubs and chef's tables that the owner, Camden, hosts frequently" —MZ

12 Xiangyang Bei Lu 襄阳北路12号
eggshanghai.com
Monday–Sunday 8am–6.30pm
¥¥¥¥

2 Highline

Recommended by Betty Richardson

"Channelling sleek 1950s SoCal vibes, this all-day lounge restaurant is where Shanghai's well-heeled young things come for hearty yet elevated American breakfasts, weekend brunches, lunches and dinners courtesy of chef Anna Bautista. Bautista's fluffy ricotta pancakes are reason enough to continue to blink your way through a hangover during the day, but an evening visit affords full advantage of the spectacular roof terrace and cosy fire pit"—BR

6F, 282 Huaihai Zhong Lu
淮海中路282号香港广场北座雅诗阁
酒店6层
+86 (0)21 6333 0176
Brunch Saturday and Sunday only,
11am–1am
¥¥¥

③ Yongnian Breakfast Market

Recommended by Betty Richardson

"At the intersection of Yongnian Lu and Shunchang Lu, between 4am and 9am, you'll catch one of Shanghai's last remaining street breakfast markets. Frequented by locals en route to work, you'll find freshly made soy bean milk (*dou jiang* 豆浆), *jianbing* (煎饼), sticky rice rolls (*cifantuan* 粢饭团), fried *youtiao* (油条) and an endless array of Chinese pastries (*shaobing* 烧饼). Don't be shy, get stuck right in and use your trusty Chinese phrase *yi ge* ('one of those')! Cash is accepted, though most sellers will prefer you scan their WeChat or Alipay payment code (see page 12) instead"—*BR*

Shunchang Lu, near Yongnian Lu • Open daily 4am–9am • ¥¥¥¥

④ Dong Tai Xiang 东泰祥

Recommended by DJ Zhang

"In Shanghai, we have crescent-shaped fried dumplings known as *guo tie* (锅贴) and also round fried dumplings known as *shengjian* with flavourful pork juice inside. This place is currently my go-to for *shengjian*: these juicy lovelies have thin skins and a supple pork filling inside with a tinge of sweetness, as has most Shanghai food. Plus, the spring onion oil noodles here are off the hook. The baby pork wonton soup (*xiao hun tun* 小馄饨) is also good"—*DJZ*

Various branches, including 188 Chongqing Bei Li (near Dagu Lu)
重庆北路188号(近大沽路)
+86 (0)21 6359 5808
Open daily 24 hours
¥¥¥

⑤ Mei Xin Dian Xin 美心点心

Recommended by DJ Zhang

"There are some things that cannot be replicated abroad; even in a city's Chinatown, dumpling dough is usually too thick and never crispy enough. But in Shanghai the fried pork dumplings (*guo tie* 锅贴) have crispy bottoms and the spring onion oil pancakes (*cong you bing* 葱油饼) have just the right thickness and amount of salt and onions"—*DJZ*

4F, Unit A22, Zhong Yi Building, 580 Nanjing Xi Lu
南京西路580号仲益大厦F幢4楼A22
+86 (0)21 6247 0030
Open daily 7am–7pm
¥¥¥

6   A Da Cong You Bing

Recommended by Jamie Barys

"Mr Wu wakes up at 5am to make his spring onion oil masterpieces, mixing the dough that will later be slathered with pork lard and stuffed with green onions before hitting the spitting-hot grill. Each batch of 20 pancakes takes about 15 minutes, including the time it takes to get a crispy finish inside the kiln hidden under the griddle, so expect long queues"—JB

4, 120 Ruijin Er Lu, by Yongjia Lu (the storefront is on Yongjia Lu)
瑞金二路120号-4
Open daily 6am–3pm
¥¥¥¥

7   100 Nanyang Lu

Recommended by Jenny Gao

"Here, at the corner of Xinkang Lu, in the morning you will often see a queue outside an unnamed storefront. This spot has been turning out some of the best sticky rice rolls (*cifantuan* 粢饭团) in the city for more than 20 years. A classic Shanghainese breakfast food, these consist of sticky rice wrapped around a fried dough stick, stewed pork and egg, pork floss and pickles, all wrapped up into a convenient portable rice ball. The lady here makes them at lightning speed and the wait is never more than 10 minutes"—JG

100 Nanyang Lu 南阳路100号
5.30am–10am (or until sold out)
¥¥¥¥

8   Xiao Tao Yuan 小桃园

Recommended by DJ Zhang

"Fried dough (*youtiao* 油条) is one of my main loves and a key ingredient in many of the dishes here. *Youtiao* can also be eaten as it is, simply dipped in soy sauce. My favourite order here is the original egg pancake roll (*yuan wei dan bing* 原味蛋饼), a huge pancake covered with a layer of egg wrapped around *youtiao*. I also love the sticky rice roll (*cifantuan* 糍饭团), because it is stuffed with plenty of *youtiao* and salted egg, which makes everything better! Lastly, add some savoury tofu pudding (*xian dou hua* 咸豆花)"—DJZ

1251 Fuxing Zhong Lu, near Xiangyang Nan Lu 复兴中路1251号-1临
+86 153 0613 9333 • Open daily 24 hours • ¥¥¥¥

9 Jianbing on Xiangyang Lu and Yongkang Lu

Recommended by Michael Zee

"A thin millet and wheat crêpe, an egg, a crispy cracker called a *buocui* (薄脆), pickles and hoisin sauce: the *jianbing* is one of China's greatest breakfasts. While there are many options on the menu at this humble street stand, all you really need to decide is if you want chilli or not. But don't sleep in too late, because at around 10.30am these ladies pack up and wheel their cart home..."—*MZ*

241 Xiangyang Lu and Yongkang Lu
在襄阳路上的煎饼
Open daily 6am–10.30am
¥¥¥¥

XIAOLONGBAO

There are few things more iconic in the world of Shanghai food than *xiaolongbao*, or soup dumplings. All across the city, you see *ayis* (literally 'aunties', a friendly term for most women in the service industry) and young men tirelessly rolling, filling and pleating, surrounded by towers of bamboo steamers and teapots filled with black vinegar for dipping.

Traditionally the soup inside the dumplings, classically made from pork gelatine, is packed with flavour, while the skin is yielding, yet robust enough not to tear accidentally. The ratio of soup-to-filling-to-skin is a hotly debated topic.

There are important local variations. Wuxi- and Nanjing-style *xiaolongbao* are fat and sweet; the Taiwanese style, precise and delicate, elevates the craft to an art form; while the Shanghai style is the workhorse, with its sturdy skin and fatty filling. Restaurants sometimes specialise in a few particular flavours, such as hairy crab, or pork with egg yolk, or they might offer a multitude of spicy Sichuan varieties.

Some restaurants offer a guide on how to eat them, knowing that first-timers can burn themselves, but as long as you're dextrous with chopsticks you won't have any problems.

A handy guide to eating *xiaolongbao*

· Gently lift the *xiaolongbao* at the 'nipple', being careful not to tear the skin, and place it on a Chinese soup spoon.

· Bite a small hole in the side and suck out the delicious hot soup.

· Dip the dumpling in vinegar, making sure some goes inside the hole.

· Pop the whole dumpling in your mouth.

· Repeat.

See also Nanjing Tangbao (page 54).

⑩ Man Long Chun 满陇春

Recommended by Michael Zee

"While many *xiaolongbao* restaurants in Shanghai have a certain rustic Communist charm, Man Long Chun offers a more refined dining experience. Don't be put off if you see a table full of social media types snapping away, the quality of the XLBs here is just as good as anywhere else in town"—*MZ*

73 Yongkang Lu 永康路73号(兴顺东里底商)
+86 139 1778 5514
Monday–Friday 11am–2.30pm, Saturday and Sunday 11.30am–3pm,
Open daily 5pm–10pm
¥¥¥

11 Fahua Tangbao
法华汤包馆

Recommended by Wei Diao

"A small place, always full of local Shanghainese. Here, people wait in line for a hand-crafted, traditional taste of their childhood"—WD

This is a very discreet restaurant; from the outside you'll just see a single window with a red banner over it. Enter via the door on the left that looks as though it's the way into someone's house. For such a small space, this place offers lots of different fillings. The fresh meat (鲜肉汤包) is the house signature, but the really interesting menu item here is the *shaomai* (烧卖), which, unlike their Cantonese cousins, are filled with rice, not pork.

504 Fahuazhen Lu
(near Xianghuaqiao Lu)
法华镇路504号(近香花桥路)
+86 (0)21 6283 4915
Open daily 6am–8.30pm
¥¥¥¥

12 Lin Long Fang 麟笼坊特色小笼包

Recommended by Camden Hauge, DJ Zhang, Jenny Gao

"There are several types of soup dumpling here. My favourites are pork and salted egg yolk dumplings (*dan huang xian rou* 蛋黄鲜肉小笼包) and extra-large pure hairy crab roe dumplings (*chun xie fen* 纯蟹粉小笼包), which cost significantly more but are totally worth it. Your cholesterol will skyrocket, so bring plenty of people to share these with. Please note: vinegar with ginger costs extra but it does make a difference; regular vinegar is free"—*DJZ*

"My go-to *xiaolongbao* restaurant for more than 10 years. They have now opened three additional branches, but I stick to the original on Jianguo Dong Lu. My order is always the same: a basket of crab roe *xiaolongbao*, a bowl of spring onion oil noodles (one of the best in Shanghai) and an egg drop seaweed soup (bland, but nice to cleanse your palate between bites). Despite the *baos* not always looking a million bucks, the flavour is superlative"—*JG*

10 Jianguo Dong Lu
建国东路10号
+86 (0)21 6386 7021
Open daily 6.30am–8.30pm
¥¥¥

13 Fu Chun 富春小笼

Recommended by Camden Hauge, Jamie Barys

"Lin Long Fang (see above) and Fu Chun are my go-tos. Fu Chun just underwent a renovation, but they still have the best pork chop noodle soup to accompany their meaty *xiaolongbao*"—*CH*

"This local institution has been serving up a taste of Shanghai-style soup dumplings with their thicker dumpling skins and sweet broth since 1959. The second floor serves other Shanghainese dishes in a sit-down setting, but the packed first floor offers quick, counter-service dining with steamer baskets constantly rotating out of the kitchen"—*JB*

650 Yuyuan Lu (near Zhenning Lu)
愚园路650号(近镇宁路)
+86 (0)21 6252 5117
Open daily 6am–12am
¥¥¥

14 Shan Shan Xiaolongbao 姗姗小笼包

Recommended by Xiaoyi Liu, Michael Zee

"This is the place where I usually get *xiaolongbao*. Tourists may be interested to know that they can deliver, too. The dumplings are always very sound and of a consistently high quality. Get the little wontons as well, as they're some of the best value in town"—XL

"I always go for a basket of the Wuxi-style *xiaolongbaos* (无锡小笼). The meat is rich and sweet, and requires plenty of black vinegar to cut through its intensity. They're also jumbo-sized compared to their Shanghai cousins, with only four in a basket. Unfortunately, the lady at the counter where you order can be a little tricky, which – as you might imagine – adds nothing but warm memories to the experience…"—MZ

749 Kangding Lu (near Jiaozhou Lu)
康定路749号(近胶州路)
+86 (0)21 6283 4915
Open daily 6am–8.30pm
¥¥¥

15 Wu You Xian 屋有鲜

Recommended by Michael Zee

"Shanghai has no shortage of 'water towns': pockets of picturesque curiosity built on canals or rivers, where locals can go and eat stinky tofu or sit by a pretty waterside and imagine what Ming or Qing dynasty China would have been like. In Zhaojialou (召稼楼), a rather unremarkable water town about 90 minutes' metro ride from central Shanghai, you will find one of the city's best *xiaolongbao* restaurants. At Wu You Xian, demand is so high that they frequently have to stop taking orders to allow the kitchen to catch up. Famous for their hairy crab XLBs, they are most busy during October when the crabs are in season. One of the few remaining cash-only eateries in the city"—MZ

2073 Zhaojialou Shendu Highway (Su Zhao Lu)
召稼楼沈杜公路2073号(苏召路)
+86 135 6486 4907
Friday–Wednesday 8am–4pm, closed Thursday
¥¥¥¥

NOODLES

Eating a bowl of noodles in China is a basic act that nevertheless taps into something elemental. Noodles are sold for the masses, for the elite, and for everyone in between. You could be hurrying through a bowl of something rich and fatty in a café that buys noodles in, or enjoying the wondrous theatre of watching a master pull the strands by hand in front of you, then throw them into scalding-hot beef soup.

Noodles have ancient origins: archeological excavations have uncovered 4,000-year-old noodles that were made from millet, a grain indigenous to China. In present-day Shanghai, the vast majority of noodles are made from wheat. The gluten in wheat allows dough to be stretched, giving a bowl of hand-pulled noodles (*lamian* 拉面) its distinctive chew. They're one of those 'get your phone ready to film' dishes: in a moment, a skein of dough transforms from one to two, to eight and – suddenly – to 128 perfect strands.

An entire guide book could be dedicated solely to the noodle shops of Shanghai, but a few rise above the rest. The vast majority lack any finesse in décor or ambience: you eat under fluorescent lighting or seated on plastic stools down a side alley, with the focus firmly on flavour, price and speed. At peak times, table turnover is fast. Noodles are one of the few Chinese foods that tend to be eaten quickly and often solo; patrons will glance at their phones, but there is no chit-chat to interfere with eating. The dishes here are simple compared to their Japanese counterparts.

Whether it's a 10RMB bowl of spring onion oil noodles, (*cong you mian* 葱油面) at Lao Di Fang Mian Guan (see page 32), or maybe crab gold noodles (蟹黄金) at Cejerdary for a handsome 360RMB (see page 31), Shanghai has a noodle for everyone.

See also Ding Te Le and Bar No. 3 (pages 50 and 110).

16 Wei Xiang Zhai 味香斋

Recommended by Jamie Barys, Cat Nelson

"This French Concession shop has been slinging sesame-peanut noodles for decades. Pay at the counter, elbow your way to a spot at a table (they're shared) and place your receipt on a numbered clothes pin for waiting staff"—*JB*

"I have a deep appreciation for places that only do one thing but totally kill it. People come for the sesame paste-doused noodles slicked with chilli oil, studded with chewy tofu and showered in chopped spring onions. It's a 10RMB affair eaten in rickety, fake wood booths and you might never be happier"—*CN*

14 Yandang Lu (near Huaihai Middle Lu) 雁荡路14号(近淮海中路)
+86 (0)21 6482 8236 • Open daily 7.30am–9pm • ¥¥¥¥

17 Gu Sha Wu Mian 谷沙屋面铺

Recommended by Betty Richardson

"Having been upgraded from an outside operation, consisting of an umbrella and a few plastic stools, popularity has propelled Gu Sha into a clean, well-run noodle institution. Their system works like a buffet. State whether you want soup noodles (*tang mian*) or dry noodles (*ban mian*, the superior choice in my opinion) and point to the toppings you want: baseball-sized pork meatballs, preserved chopped greens with pork, sticky sweet ribs, 'red braised' pork belly or tofu rolls"—*BR*

1011 Qiu Jiang Lu 虬江路1011号格林联盟酒店旁 • *+86 (0)21 5663 2425*
Monday–Friday 5.30am–2pm, Saturday and Sunday 5am–10am • ¥¥¥¥

18 Liu Tang Men 六樘门

Recommended by Jamie Barys

"Spicy Sichuan noodles don't get much better than those they serve here. An ageing member of a Chengdu rock band started the place back in the day, replacing his hair-raising guitar riffs with tongue-tingling spice mixtures. The world-famous dan dan noodles are great, but try the cowpea and minced pork spicy noodles (碗杂面) for something new"—*JB*

419-1 Xinhua Lu (near Dingxi Lu)
新华路419号-1(香花桥路)
+86 131 2231 4059
Open daily 7am–9.30pm
¥¥¥¥

19 Cejerdary (*Xie Jia Da Yuan*) 蟹家大院

Recommended by Jenny Gao

"My favourite two bowls of noodles in Shanghai are here. Cejerdary is a now-iconic restaurant that only has two items on the menu: a 72RMB bowl of hairy crab noodles and a 360RMB bowl of hairy crab noodles. Ironically, the place is run by a vegetarian monk who has never tasted his own food. Each bowl requires the hand-picked meat and roe of 12 crabs and the 360RMB bowl is topped with edible gold. The latter may be one of the most ludicrous but delicious bites I've ever put in my mouth"—*JG*

1266 Kai Xuan Lu (near Anshun Lu)
凯旋路1266号(近安顺路)
+86 (0)21 5230 0008
Open daily 11am–8.30pm
¥¥¥¥

20   Yi Mian Chun Feng 一面春风

Recommended by Xiaoyi Liu

"A modern noodle house in the former French Concession. This is not your regular Shanghainese- or Suzhou-style noodle, mushy and overcooked. Instead, they source the noodles from a factory that also produces Japanese ramen. They are something between ramen and Chinese white noodles: slightly springy and chewy. Here, the noodle soup is made from six different kinds of mushroom, so for people who prefer a traditional taste it's not the best choice. I prefer the dry noodles (*ban mian*), that are without soup, just noodles with toppings. My favourite is double dragon *ban mian* (双龙拌面), with a topping made of pork slices, young Chinese chives and eel, best enjoyed during eel season (late spring to early autumn). Pork lardo rice (猪油拌饭) is also strongly recommended, where you are served a bowl of rice accompanied with a small cube of pork lardo and soy sauce"—*XL*

26 Wuxing Lu
吴兴路26号
+86 (0)21 6467 5517
Open daily 11am–4pm and 5pm–9.30pm
¥¥¥

21   Lao Di Fang Mian Guan 老地方面馆

Recommended by Michael Zee

"At 6.30am, the Old Noodle Place has a queue out of the door and down the street. Patrons slurp their noodles with voracious speed and leave. At 11.30am the queue picks up again for the lunch-time rush. My personal favourite here is the *zhajianmian* (炸酱面), noodles topped with minced pork and fermented soy bean paste, with a deep-fried pork chop (*zha pai* 炸排) if you're feeling particularly hungry"—*MZ*

233 Xiangyang Bei Lu (near Yongkang Lu)
襄阳北路233号(近永康路)
+86 (0)21 6471 0556
Monday–Friday 6.30am–10am, 11am–2pm and 5pm–7pm, Saturday and Sunday 6.30am–10am and 11am–2pm
¥¥¥

22 Henan La Mian 河南拉面

Recommended by Betty Richardson

"Henan La Mian caters to homesick workers from – you guessed it – Henan, and the noodles are distinctly different from Shanghai styles. My favourite is *chao dao xiao ban mian* (超刀削拌面), thick, knife-pared noodles sheared from a huge dough block into boiling water, then furiously stir-fried on a street-side wok with greens and savoury sauce. Add chilli oil and, if you want to get really local, peel a clove of raw garlic and munch it while eating your noodles"—*BR*

114 Zhaozhou Lu (near Ji'an Lu) 肇周路114弄1号(近易买得)
+86 (0)21 6355 4118 • Monday–Friday 24 hours, closed Saturday and Sunday
¥¥¥¥

As the most populous city in the world, there are a lot of hungry mouths to feed in Shanghai, all the time.

This chapter is dedicated to daytime eating, between meals, from vendors that offer limited or no seating. So if you've missed the *jianbing* (煎饼) lady at breakfast, or you're still peckish after lunch, these places are for you.

Whether it's something relatively local to Shanghai, such as a *shao jin yin bing* (烧缙云饼) from neighbouring Zhejiang province, or a bite from further afield such as a piece of Taiwanese fried chicken or a juicy Xinjiang lamb skewer (*xin jiang shao chuar* 新疆烤串), the Shanghainese love a snack. You may stumble upon a 'snack shop' (*ling shi dian* 零食店), a classic pick 'n' mix selection of vacuum-packed chicken parts and sugary candy of unknown flavours.

To Western tastes, many of the choices here can be disappointing. However, some snack shops will have a deli counter or fresh snack section on the street, serving hot fresh Suzhou-style pork moon cakes (*suzhou xian rou yue bing* 苏州鲜肉月饼), or *qing tuan* (青团), a sticky green rice cake popular around the time of the Tomb Sweeping Festival.

As always in any city the world over, a long queue is an encouraging indication of the quality of what's on offer.

See also Pudong Muslim Market (page 124).

23 Lao Shi Cong You Bing 老式葱油饼

Recommended by Michael Zee

"At this address, there are two snack vendors, one in green and the other in red. The former has a standard breakfast stall offering *youtiao* and soy milk. But the man in red, he makes *rou jia mo* (肉夹馍), also known as Chinese hamburgers. The fatty pork (*wu hua rou* 五花肉) is to die for"—MZ

211 Taixing Lu
泰兴路211号
Open daily 5.30am–7pm
¥¥¥¥

24 Yang's Dumplings 小杨生煎包

Recommended by Michael Zee

"All Shanghai will scream at me for putting Yang's in this guide, but I've never seen a branch empty; the dumplings are bloody delicious! The dumpling skin is unleavened and they have lots of soup. Aside from the traditional pork, they also have prawn and shepherd's purse (a green leafy vegetable) and you can order a selection plate of two of each. Winner-winner *shengjian* dinner. Order at the counter, take your ticket to the window and give it to the staff"—*MZ*

Various locations, including 486 Zhejiang Middle Lu 浙江中路486号
+86 (0)21 6350 2279
Monday–Friday 7am–9pm, closed Saturday and Sunday • ¥¥¥¥

25 Peng Yuan Guo Tie 朋缘锅贴/洋洋

Recommended by Jamie Barys

"This teeny former French Concession stall might not look like much, but the husband-and-wife team serve the best fried dumplings in the city. If you get there early enough, you can sometimes get their *shengjianbao* (breakfast soup dumplings, with thicker skins), too. The potstickers are wrapped to order throughout the day, so you always get the freshest dumplings"—JB

102 Gao'an Lu (near Zhaojiabang Lu)
高安路102号(近肇嘉浜路)
Open daily 6am–5pm
¥¥¥¥

26 Jin Yun Shao Bing 缙云烧饼

Recommended by Michael Zee

"In Chinese cooking, there are a lot of different types of *shao bing*, meaning almost any baked cake, bread or biscuit that is vaguely round. This small shop front makes *Jin Yun shao bing* (缙云烧饼). (Jinyun is a county in the neighbouring Zhejiang province.) A thin pork-and-pepper-filled pancake is cooked in a tandoor oven until crisp. If you get one freshly made, be careful when it's handed to you: it will be extremely hot, so don't drop it!"—MZ

490 Huashan Lu
华山路490号
Open daily 9am–10pm
¥¥¥¥

27 Yi Ren Yi Guo *Guo Tie Wang* 一人一锅锅贴王

Recommended by DJ Zhang

"These fried pork dumplings (*guo tie* 锅贴) are the 'extra' version of those at Lao Shi Cong You Bing (see page 35), as they have an additional crispy layer at the bottom! This place also has baby pork wonton soup (*xiaohuntun* 小馄饨), featuring wontons with delicate skins"—DJZ

Unit 1, 228 Zhizaoju Lu
制造局路228-1号临
Open daily 6am–9pm
¥¥¥¥

28 Da Hu Chun Qijiandian 大壶春旗舰店

Recommended by Michael Zee

"While many might suggest Yang's (see page 36) for *shengjianbao*, I know locals who would say that this is the more traditional of the two: the dumplings contain less soup, have fluffier skins and are overall less salty. The interior of the flagship branch looks like someone has actually put some thought into it. Considering the *shengjianbao* here are only 8RMB per portion, why don't you try both places and see what you think?"—*MZ*

136 Sichuan Middle Lu
四川中路136号
+86 (0)21 6313 0155
Open daily 6.30am–7pm
¥¥¥¥

29 Bian Jie Dan Bing 卞姐蛋饼

Recommended by Michael Zee

"If you managed to sleep in and miss out on a *jianbing*, then fear not. *Dan bing* 蛋饼, or egg pancake, is the *jianbing*'s near cousin and just as delicious. The main difference is that, halfway through cooking, the whole thing is flipped over, so that the egg is on the outside and – even better – they're available all day long"—*MZ*

192 Shaanxi Nan Lu
陕西南路192
Open daily 7am–7pm
¥ ¥ ¥ ¥

30 Xian Mo Rou Jia Mo 鲜馍肉夹馍

Recommended by Michael Zee

"The *rou jia mo* makers here not only put together superb classic fatty pork 'hamburgers', but they are thinking of all of you who happen to be on a diet, too, with a lean pork version also on the menu. With a giant cleaver, the staff cut open bread and generously fill it with juicy meat. Expect a crowd of hungry locals and expats at most times of the day"—*MZ*

175 Dongzhu'anbang Lu
东诸安浜路175号
+86 138 1634 1114
Open daily 12pm–7.30pm
¥ ¥ ¥ ¥

31 Wuhan Three Delicacies Tofu Skin
Wuhan San Xian Dou Pi 武汉三鲜豆皮

Recommended by Michael Zee

"Follow the Yangtze river far enough upstream from Shanghai and you eventually reach Wuhan (武汉), where this street snack hails from. A layer of tofu skin is topped with a layer of rice and finished with ham and more beancurd. It is then fried in a giant pan until crispy, carefully flipped over and cut into smallish squares. Texture is just as important as taste with this popular snack, and don't forget to add some chilli sauce"—*MZ*

442 Guangxi North Lu 广西北路442号
Open daily 7am–10am • ¥¥¥¥

SWEETS

China is not typically known for sugary treats. Visitors can be surprised by the lack of desserts on menus; instead, a plate of watermelon or orange segments often finishes off a vast banquet or hot pot. You might even discover that any desserts you do find are lacking sweetness. While sugar consumption in Shanghai is growing, the Chinese consume on average nine times less sugar than their American counterparts.

In recent years, the city has seen an explosion of imported sweet delights, from gimmicky Japanese candies to small-batch Italian gelato that – in some instances – cleverly fuse traditional techniques with contemporary Chinese flavours.

Apart from this new generation of bakeries, patisseries and ice cream shops, the Shanghainese relish the successive waves of fruit that come into season throughout the year. In the summer, in fruit shops (水果店), you see trays of pomelo (柚子), the largest of all citrus, its pith carefully removed by patient *ayis*. Another refreshing treat is sour plum juice (酸梅汤), consumed for its medicinal properties. In the colder months, small hawthorn apples (*shanzha* 山楂) are served on a stick and covered in crunchy sugar, a combination of incredibly tart and sweet flavours.

A brief guide to seasonal fruit in Shanghai

- January: citrus (especially mandarins), sugar cane (as fresh-pressed juice)

- March–April: peaches, strawberries (grown in the city)

- June: *yangmei* (tart-tasting, reminiscent of strawberry and rhubarb), watermelons (often sold by the half or quarter, with a spoon), lychees and longans

- July–August: mangoes, mangosteens, pears

See also Commune Social, Shanghailander (Coffee Bar) and Bee Cheng Hiang (pages 84, 98 and 129).

㉜ Luneurs Boulanger + Glacier

Recommended by Michael Zee, Betty Richardson

"What Luneurs does well is indulgence. Sure, the sourdough bread and baguettes they bake here are great. But what everyone comes for are the next-level pastries – a croissant that ticks all the boxes, and fabulous cakes – and the ice cream. With no space for laptops, most customers also come to enjoy a moment of serenity" —MZ

67 Xingfu Lu, Block E, Number 107
幸福路67号E座107号
Tuesday–Sunday 8am–8pm, closed Monday
¥¥¥¥

33 Pan Yong Xing Rice Desserts 潘甬兴糕点

Recommended by Betty Richardson

"If you've got a sweet tooth and a sense of adventure, then Pan Yong Xing's plethora of Chinese sweet treats make for an ideal between-meal snack. The best, in my opinion, are spongy and fragrant fermented osmanthus wine rice cakes (*guihuajiu niangao*), although the vibrant green, sesame filled stuffed coin cakes (*xianjinbing*) run them a close second"—*BR*

52 Nanhui Lu 南汇路52号梅龙镇广场后门对面
+86 139 1751 3893
Open daily 6am–10pm
¥¥¥¥

34 Strictly Cookies

Recommended by Jamie Barys, Michael Zee

"A magnet for expats. While classic choc chip is a winner, they get inventive with a flavour of the month – think coconut and Chinese bayberry (*yangmei*), or lime crunch – and you must try the sweet-and-savoury Snack Pack"—*JB*

"My favourites are the Snack Pack – with pretzels, salty potato chips and caramel baked into the cookie for salty-sweet perfection – and the Ginger Blast. Find a special edition Milk and Cereal cookie at Egg (see page 15)"—*MZ*

1F Metrobank Plaza, Room 103, 1166 Yan'an Lu West (near Panyu Lu)
延安西路1166号103室(延东北人往小区里走)
strictlycookies.com • +86 156 1803 8503
Monday–Saturday 9am–5.30pm, closed Sunday • ¥¥¥¥

35 MBD

Recommended by Xiaoyi Liu

"Opened by Hiro San, the first chief baker of Farine (a legendary bakery in the French Concession, now closed), MBD combines all that is best from a French boulangerie with Japanese craftsmanship. It's the perfect neighbourhood bakery, where people go to buy loaves of French bread and enjoy croissants as well as creative Japanese-style breads. They also sell a small selection of natural wines on the side"—*XL*

785-3 Huashan Lu 华山路785-3
+86 186 1633 2255
Tuesday–Sunday 8am–7pm, closed Monday
¥¥¥¥

36 Pain Chaud *Xuhui*

Recommended by Michael Zee

"The new flagship Pain Chaud on the corner of Jiashan and Jianguo Xi Lu shows that the company is ambitious, and they still do one thing really *really* well. Some of Shanghai's best French pastries, cakes and petits fours"—*MZ*

256 Jianguo Xi Lu
建国西路256号
+86 (0)21 3356 0520
Open daily 7.30am–9.30pm
¥¥¥¥

37 Gelato dal Cuore *Da Ke Rui Bingqilin* 达可芮冰淇淋

Recommended by Betty Richardson

"For times when only the real deal will do, Gelato dal Cuore is there to tempt me from the dietary straight and narrow with its frozen peaks of the finest Italian gelato. My favourite flavours include coffee with almonds, black sesame and tiramisu. See also the thick Italian-style hot chocolate: an ideal counterpoint to the inevitable 'brain freeze'"—*BR*

600-9 Shaanxi Bei Lu 陕西北路600号-9
facebook.com/gelatodalcuore • +86 (0)21 6148 1388
Open daily 12pm–9pm
¥¥¥¥

㊳ Huangjin Shou Si Mianbao 黄金手撕面包

Recommended by Michael Zee

"Immediately next door to the Avocado Lady (see page 125), this small bakery of traditional Chinese breads and biscuits is often overlooked by those on the search for more contemporary sourdoughs and expensive artisanal pastries. My favourites are the 'meaty baby' *rousong beibei* (肉松贝贝), a cream bun topped with pork floss (a flavour combination I cannot get enough of) and also a bag of the sesame and pine nut cookies (*zhima bing* 芝麻饼), which are lightly sweet and work perfectly with cheese and a glass of wine"—*MZ*

272-1 Wulumuqi Middle Lu 乌鲁木齐中路272-1
Open daily 6am until sold out • ¥¥¥¥

EARLY & LATE

Sadly, in recent years, China has seen its street food and night market scene diminish considerably. The government has been tough about removing illegal vendors in an attempt to clean up the city's image, as the public becomes more concerned with food hygiene and provenance.

Long gone are the days of pedlars on every pavement, mobile carts making fried rice at midnight, or chairs on a street corner serving skewers to hungry teenagers. But these 'small bites' (*xiao chi* 小吃) have not disappeared completely.

Compared to many other cities in Asia, you might be mistaken for thinking that Shanghai has limited late-night options when it comes to delicious food. Wandering the streets of the former French Concession in the small hours can feel like a lost cause, with your night finishing in a Lawson or Family Mart convenience store (all the city's locals have been there at some point).

But Shanghai is good at keeping secrets.

A speakeasy-style doorway might lead to a family-run, 24-hour hole-in-the-wall churning out yellow croaker noodles, or pork chops with sweet vinegar. Almost half of Shanghai's 24 million residents are migrants from other regions of China, so, whether it's a group of street sweepers yet to start their shift, or a taxi driver just finishing his night, you can count on sharing a table with an eclectic group.

Out in the hinterlands of the city, in a car park in Hongqiao perhaps (see page 51), you can find drunk businessmen gorging on kimchi hot pot and fried chicken; though in their cases the tasty food is a mere sponge for the alcohol.

See also Dong Tai Xiang, Henan La Mian and Convenience Stores (pages 19, 33 and 127).

39 Cha's *Cha Canting* 查餐厅

Recommended by Betty Richardson

"As either a late-night guilty pleasure or for prudent hangover prevention, Cha's comforting Hong Kong eats are consistently delicious whichever way you look at them. The original location has a charmingly worn patina, making the place a real everyman's diner which transports you right into a Wong Kar-wai movie. Essential orders include silky scrambled eggs with shrimp, beef ho fun noodles, peanut butter French toast, BBQ pork instant noodles, pineapple buns stuffed with chilled butter, and gloriously creamy iced milk tea"—*BR*

1/F 30 Sinan Lu 思南路30号
+86 (0)21 6093 2062 • Open daily 11am–1.30am
¥¥¥¥

40 Ding Te Le 顶特勒粥面馆

Recommended by Jamie Barys, Michael Zee

"This 24-hour congee and noodle joint is tucked away inside a neighbourhood alleyway (*nongtang*). Their Shanghainese vibe is reason enough to visit, but the noodles (and a killer pork chop) keep you coming back for more"—*JB*

"You might surprise the staff by rocking up at 4am for noodles, but they are exceptionally friendly. Order the spicy pork noodles (辣肉素浇面) or the white sauce onion and pork noodles (白汁葱油肉丝拌面) but always, always with a pork chop on the side. Absolutely fantastic"—*MZ*

Lane 22, 494 Huai Hai Middle Lu 淮海中路494弄22号(工商银行旁)
+86 (0)21 5103 6275 • Open daily 24 hours • ¥¥¥

41 Fukuchan Fu Kao Jin Hua 福烤锦花

Recommended by Camden Hauge

"I wouldn't classify myself as an early bird; instead, I have to rely on late-night food as I usually finish a shift at my restaurant around or after midnight. My favourite spot for these early-hours meals is this smoky, authentic hole-in-the-wall Japanese yakitori spot. There's nothing better at 1am, I promise; try it yourself and see"—CH

223 Changle Lu
长乐路223号(近陕西南路)
+86 (0)21 5403 6270
Open daily 5am–2am
¥¥¥¥

42 Jini Dapaidang 吉尼大排档

Recommended by Jenny Gao

"A trusty late-night favourite. My friends and I call it the 'red tent', because you basically sit under a large tent in the parking lot of a strip mall out in the Hongqiao hinterlands. It's filled with red-faced salarymen and groups of rowdy kids hunched over platters of fried chicken and bubbling vats of kimchi hot pot. It's hot, it's loud, it's lawless and – to be honest – the vibe probably makes the food taste better than it actually is. But who am I kidding, you're here to get sloshed more than anything. So order a giant trough of Asahi, some fried chicken, seafood pancakes and the kimchi hot pot with spam, sausages, rice cakes and tofu. Don't forget to ask them to throw an instant ramen on top"—JG

Lane 1, 1101 Hongquan Lu (near Hongxin Lu)
虹泉路1101弄1号(近虹莘路)
+86 138 1655 4282
Open daily 4pm–4am
¥¥¥¥

43 Ajiya Yakiniku

Recommended by Betty Richardson

"An institution that has only matured with age and grown in popularity, Ajiya is where locals and Japanese expats come to decompress over hot coal barbecues laden with the juiciest cuts of meat, as well as copious flagons of Suntory whiskey highballs. I like to order all-beef here, since the quality is excellent for the price, along with a bowl or two of the egg yolk-topped 'special rice' and chilled noodles with cucumber, shiso leaf and salted plum. With a fun, upbeat atmosphere that carries on until 2am on weekdays, Ajiya is my sure bet for easy-going group dinners"—*BR*

4/F, 1333 Huai Hai Middle Lu
淮海中路1333号4楼
+86 (0)21 5425 1723
Monday–Friday 5pm–2am, Saturday and Sunday 5pm–12am
¥¥¥¥

44 Nanjing Tangbao 南京汤包

Recommended by Michael Zee

"OK, so the dumplings themselves might not be the greatest in town, but the Boss (*laoban*) of this small late night *xiaolongbao* restaurant requests a photo with every visitor *and* wants to know where you're from. It's the generous hospitality you find here that will keep you coming back for more"—*MZ*

641 Jianguo Xi Lu
建国西路641号
+86 (0)21 6473 5648
Open daily 5am–2.30am
¥¥¥

45 Hai Di Lao 海底捞火锅 (北京西路店)

Recommended by Cat Nelson

"Since I moved to China a decade ago, this 24-hour chain from Sichuan has been a mainstay in my late-night dining rotation. It made its name by having fabulous service in a country where that's usually a second thought at best: snacks while you wait, free manicures, lens cloths for steamed-up glasses. All alongside spicy, numbing Sichuan hot pot and a great sauce bar, making for a total winner"—*CN*

Various locations, including 3/F, 1068 Beijing Xi Lu (near Jiangning Lu)
北京西路1068号食博汇3层(近江宁路)
+86 (0)21 6258 9758 • Open daily 24 hours • ¥¥¥

46 Beijing Mutton Hot Pot
Yi Pin Ju Reqi Yangrou Guan 一品居热气羊肉馆

Recommended by Michael Zee

"True Beijingers would lament this style of hot pot, but it is as authentic as it gets. The meat is never pre-frozen and butchering takes place out on the street, it's not a marketing gimmick. Chinese medicine recommends eating mutton in autumn and winter, when it's at its best. Order a round of cooked skewers to feast on while the thick slices of mutton are bubbling away"—*MZ*

352 Wulumuqi Middle Lu 乌鲁木齐中路352号
+86 (0)21 6471 5147 • Open daily 10.30am–3am
¥¥¥

47 Fei Zai Man 肥仔文澳门猪骨煲

Recommended by Michael Zee, Betty Richardson

"The name of this restaurant translates as 'Fatty Boy Wen'. As you enter, fish tanks full of all sorts of strange and wonderful shellfish await their fate. The menu is broadly Macanese-inspired without being rigid. Try any of the fish dishes prepared in Typhoon Shelter style and a few of the claypot rice dishes, making sure to get all the crunchy rice off the bottom of the pot"—*MZ*

77 Nanhui Lu 南汇路77号
+86 (0)21 6253 6777
Open daily 11am–4.30am
¥¥¥¥

HOT POT

There is truly something for everyone at a table with a bubbling hot pot in the middle.

Hot pots come in many guises, from the famed Sichuan style, bursting with lip smacking *má là* spices (麻辣) and flavours so intricately layered, to the more delicate Taiwanese-style affair at Wulao Health Elixir (see page 60). This features a light tofu broth, with a myriad of nuts or dried mushrooms, that feels both complex and uplifting.

Hot pot is not just eaten in the colder months. Despite the oppressively hot Shanghai summers, traditional Chinese medicine recommends using warming foods such as chilli to drive out 'dampness' within the body, in order to maintain health. So sitting around a bubbling cauldron of oil in the 40°C heat remains a popular pastime.

If you are with a group of four or more friends, then hot pot is an excellent idea for dinner. One person should be designated to take control, keeping a watchful eye on the thinly sliced meats, taking care that they aren't over-cooked, distributing morsels to other diners, and maintaining some semblance of decorum. That being said, one of the pleasures of a hot pot is finding a stray fish ball or piece of pumpkin bobbing around in the broth at the end of the meal, when it has become richly imbued with the flavour of the pot.

It is advisable not to wear your Sunday best when going for a hot pot, as your clothes will carry the memory of the meal home with you.

See also Hai Di Lao and Beijing Mutton Hot Pot (page 54).

48 Qimin *Qi Min Shi Ji* 齐民市集

Recommended by Michael Zee

"You should never underestimate restaurants in malls in China. Nestled deep within the Reel Mall in Jing'an, Qimin is a star among all the hot pot places in Shanghai. Chic marble banquet tables with individual hot pots allow for everyone to have what they want. Also, all the meat and vegetables are organic and imported from Taiwan"—MZ

4F, Reel Mall, 1601 Nanjing West Lu 南京西路1601号芮欧百货4层
+86 (0)21 6259 3004
Monday–Friday 11am–2pm and 5pm–10pm, Saturday and Sunday
11am–10pm • ¥¥¥¥

49 Wu Chu *Wu Chu Huoguo* 五厨火锅

Recommended by Wei Diao

"Sichuan hot pot usually comes with messy tables and a definite fragrance. But Wu Chu has a clean interior design, while the familiar hot pot aromas are present, but not as strongly as in other Sichuan hot pot restaurants. Ingredients are fresh and stocks are tasty. They have a small organic garden, vegetables from which you can order directly to your table"—*WD*

3F, 96 Plaza, 796 Dongfang Lu
东方路796号96广场3楼
+86 (0)21 6330 6887
Open daily 10am–11pm
¥¥¥¥

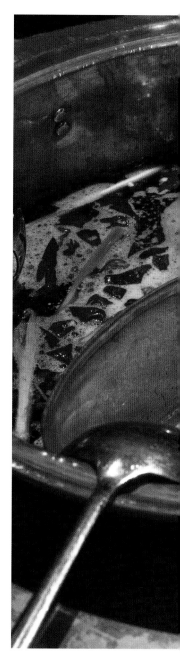

50 Wulao Health Elixir *Ding Wang Wulao Guo*
鼎王无老锅

Recommended by Camden Hauge, Jamie Barys, Cat Nelson

"I'm a hot pot purist; I only go to this place, which uses super-fresh organic ingredients, including free-flow porous 'bread' tofu and excellent service. The tofu-based broth is clean and delicious enough to drink on its own"—CH

"A humble-bragging sign by the sauce bar warns diners that the broth is so excellent that they don't recommend dipping the meat or veg into anything else. Get the collagen hot pot and enjoy the free-flow 'bread' tofu and probiotic frozen desserts. So delicious, you won't realise they're good for you"—JB

"I'm obsessed with spice and surprised by my own love for this mild, subtle hot pot. The meal finishes with an icy shot of Yakult-flavoured slushie. Expect a wait if you visit during normal dinner hours"—CN

2 Hengshan Lu
衡山路2号甲香樟花园内
+86 (0)21 5456 1489
Open daily 11am–2am
¥¥¥¥

51 Holy Cow *Niuniu Huoguo* 牛牛火锅

Recommended by Jamie Barys

"This organic hot pot restaurant serves farm-to-table produce and specialises in beef. The soup here is so good, you'll want to turn the gas off after you've eaten all the dipping accoutrements and go spoon-first into the big bowls of reviving broth"—JB

Room 302A, Building 1, 341 Tianshan Lu, near Weining Lu.
天山路341号缤谷文化休闲广场西区3层302A
+86 (0)21 5297 9937
Open daily 10.30am–11pm
¥¥¥¥

52 Zhen Xian Wei Zhu 真鲜围煮

Recommended by Xiaoyi Liu

"My favourite spot for Hong Kong-style hot pot, in a newly opened *shikumen* development near West Nanjing Lu. It is allegedly a copycat of a place in Hong Kong, but local diners are not that interested in any feud between restaurants, as long as the food is decent! Expect fresh seafood hot pot feasts with an array of delicious Hong Kong street food, such as chicken feet and curry fish balls"—XL

Room 201, 277 Maoming North Lu
茂名北路277号201室
+86 (0)21 6277 7277
Open daily 11am–2.30pm and 5.30pm–3am
¥¥¥

53 Halloween Hot Pot
Chihuo Xiao Yao Fu Xie Wa Huoguo
吃货小妖府蟹蛙火锅

Recommended by Michael Zee

"If you're a fan of Halloween, and if you like spicy food all year round, then this is the restaurant for you. Entering here is like stepping into a haunted house rollercoaster. Tables are decorated with cobwebs and motion-activated ghouls and the menu items are delightfully themed in their descriptions. For groups of six or more, you can also dine in their haunted tree"—MZ

2F, No.16, Lane 193 Maoming North Lu
茂名北路193弄16号丰盛里二楼
+86 (0)21 6148 8278
Open daily 11am–2.30am
¥¥¥¥

CLASSIC SHANGHAI

The distinctive flavour of Shanghai is a collision of two styles: the first is a culmination of the tastes of the surrounding provinces, predominantly Jiangsu and Zhejiang, known as home-style Shanghainese food (*ben bang cai* 本帮菜); the second is the Shanghainese fondness for cooking foods from outside China: *hai pai* (海派).

Sugar is a key ingredient in the food of the city, especially when combined with dark salty soy sauce to form a cornerstone of Shanghainese cuisine known as 'red' cooking (*hong shao* 红烧). At one of China's most recommended restaurants, Old Jesse (see right), the must-order dish is red-cooked pork (*hong shao rou* 红烧肉), a dish that is found on many menus across the city.

Dishes may come 'drunken' – marinated and cooked in rice wine – and everything from chicken, pork and crab to tofu is given the boozy treatment.

There is a liberal use of vinegar for sourness, Zhenjiang (镇江香醋) being the most popular type, used both as a cooking ingredient in dishes and as a condiment for dumplings, to cut through the fattiness of the pork.

Meanwhile, at classic city noodle restaurants, you'll always find Shanghai-style breaded pork cutlets (*zhu pai mian* 猪排面), a perfect example of the *hai pai* style of cooking; don't forget to add them to your order.

See also Ding Te Le (page 50).

54 Old Jesse *Lao Ji Shi Jiu Jia* 老吉士酒家

Recommended by Jamie Barys, Cat Nelson

"The best darn Shanghainese in town. Avoid the 'New' Jesses you see, they're not nearly as good. Call ahead to request the 'secret' menu, with such gems as the opium fish head, which requires pre-ordering days in advance"—*JB*

"Old Jesse has become one of my all-time favourites; if I could go there once a week I would (but it's too busy). Nothing I've eaten there is less than great and the Old Shanghai vibes and gruff service kill it. Get roast cod head under spring onions and the off-menu rice cakes with shepherd's purse (荠菜年糕)"—*CN*

41 Tianping Lu, near Huaihai Middle Lu 天平路41号
+86 (0)21 6282 9260 • Open daily 11am–4pm and 5.30pm–12am • ¥¥¥¥

55 Jianguo328
建国328小馆

Recommended by Betty Richardson

"The ultimate Shanghainese canteen, Jianguo328 is a *xiaoguan* (small eatery) I depend on for Shanghai eats when I don't have a group large enough to visit Old Jesse (see page 63). Their spring onion oil noodles are some of the most esteemed in Shanghai, though I can't leave without ordering the classic chopped vegetable stir-fried rice with amaranth (*jicai caifan*) and unctuous red-braised pork belly"—*BR*

328 Jianguo Xi Lu
建国西路328号
+86 (0)21 6471 3819
Open daily 11am–9.30pm
¥¥

56 Fu1088 福1088

Recommended by Camden Hauge

"Fu1088 is my perfect Shanghainese restaurant. Set in an Art Deco villa with a warren of private rooms, it serves upscale, well-made Shanghainese classics. The hand-picked crab – when in season – served with brioche sticks, and their jewel-like red-braised pork (*hong shao rou*), are my favourites"—*CH*

375 Zhenning Lu
镇宁路375号
+86 (0)21 5239 7878
Open daily 11am–2pm and 5.30pm–11pm
¥¥¥¥

57 Shang Zhi Jiao Can Shi 上只角餐室

Recommended by Xiaoyi Liu

"Authentic Shanghainese food with a lighter approach in a modern French bistro setting. Clean, fresh and affordable, it's quickly becoming a favourite among local diners. I recommend the *zao bo dou* (糟钵斗), an appetiser of pork tongue, tile fish, duck tongue and chicken in a sauce of fermented wine residue, a traditional local delight enjoyed in the summer. Seafood steamed egg is also not to be missed. Mushy pork slice (烂糊肉丝) is a home-style dish made of napa cabbage and pork slice that goes very well with a bowl of rice"—*XL*

175-4 Changle Lu 长乐路175-4号 • +86 (0)21 6387 1777
Monday–Thursday and Sunday 10.30am–12am, Friday and Saturday 10.30am–2am • ¥¥¥¥

58 Ren He Guan 人和馆

Recommended by Cat Nelson

"Excellent casual Shanghai food in somewhat kitschy, but ultimately endearing digs kitted out with 1930s Old Shanghai décor. All the classics – *hong shao rou* and the rest – have the restaurant jam-packed every evening come peak dinnertime at about 7pm"—*CN*

407 Zhaojiabang Lu 肇嘉浜路407号
+86 (0)21 6403 0731
Monday–Thursday 11am–2pm and 5pm–9.30pm, Friday–Sunday 11am–2pm and 4.30pm–9.30pm
¥¥¥¥

59 Old Style Ningbo *Jiu Kuan Ningbo Fandian*
旧款宁波饭店

Recommended by Alex Xu, Cat Nelson

"My grandparents are from Ningbo and my family always stop in here for dinner over Chinese New Year. Many Shanghainese have ancestry in Ningbo, so the cuisine of this coastal city has informed much of what we think of as 'Shanghainese' food today. Be ready, this place is a real dingy hole-in-the-wall! My favourites include: spring rolls filled with yellow croaker and shepherd's purse, red-braised pork with dried fish and squid, fried yellow croaker in a dried seaweed batter, crispy bamboo shoots with prawns and duck ham, air-dried sea eel (*man xiang*), drunken crab, razor clams, fried rice with greens and salted ham… I could go on and on. Pro tip: no corkage means you can bring your own wine"—*AX*

"The main reason to come to this hole-in-the-wall Ningbo spot is the truly exceptional fried bamboo slivers with duck ham, prawns and gingko nuts. A light showering of sugar gives it an addictive salty-sweet profile"—*CN*

Huamin Century Plaza, 660 Yan'an West Lu 延安西路660号华敏世纪广场
Open daily 11am–10pm • ¥¥¥¥

60 Rui Fu Yuan 瑞福园

Recommended by Alex Xu

"Small wontons in yellow croaker broth, crispy rice cakes, spring rolls, *shengjianbao*, fried yellow croaker in a dried seaweed batter… This is a place I go to with my parents when I'm looking for the Shanghainese delicacies and snacks that I grew up eating. The batter on the yellow croaker is wafer-thin and crisp, while the skins on the wontons have just enough spring and chew to give textural contrast. Crispy rice cakes – my sister's favourite – used to be sold on street corners everywhere; when you can find them today they are often dense and the rice has been cooked to a mush so it keeps its shape while frying. Rui Fu Yuan's have perfectly formed, individual grains of rice with a balance of chew and give, that eats much lighter, emphasising the crisp outer layer. The quality speaks for itself, as does the view when you walk in and see the tables filled with older Shanghainese uncles and aunties"—*AX*

132 Maoming South Lu
茂名南路132号
+86 (0)21 6445 8999
Open daily 11am–2pm and 5pm–9.30pm
¥¥¥¥

61 Yuan Yuan 圆苑

Recommended by Wei Diao

"This place has been at the forefront of Shanghai cuisine for decades, yet it is not hide-bound, it still keeps updating its menus several times a year. Though it is traditionally Shanghainese, you can see the influence of the younger generation in the food and décor, as well as the good service. Private rooms are available by reservation only"—WD

201 Xingguo Lu, near Tai'an Lu
兴国路201号, 近泰安路
+86 (0)21 6433 9123
Open daily 11am–10pm
¥¥¥

Shanghai has absolutely no trouble with casual. Strolling around the streets, you will see many elderly locals out for a midday walk in their pyjamas or even their underwear (switching to quilted thermal pyjamas in the winter), without as much as a hint of embarrassment.

This is reflected in the city's approach to casual dining. It's all about no-frills, no reservations, no napkins, brightly lit, Lazy Susan-spinning, *baijiu* swilling, mega-sized canteen-style restaurants. How refreshing.

In contrast, a burgeoning young middle class with an ample disposable income has been driving a demand for dining that is slightly more stylish, discerning and – more importantly – on trend. There is now a slough of moody, intimate and concept-driven eateries to choose from.

At Xime (see page 77), you might come across a table of Chinese social media influencers (*wang hong* 网红) hunting for the latest Weibo-worthy dish, while feasting on Scotch eggs with a Japanese twist and drinking home-made sochu infused with creative flavour combinations.

From Guizhou-influenced small plates in an *izakaya* setting at Oha (see page 74), to inventive, seasonal and thoughtful vegetarian dishes at Wu Guan Tang (see page 73) – a restaurant run by Buddhist monks – there is a new generation of young restaurateurs shaking things up.

See also Egg, Highline, Man Long Chun, Ajiya Yakiniku, Fei Zai Man, Homeslice, The Cannery and Pirata (pages 15, 16, 23, 52, 55, 80, 81 and 84).

62 Together 愚舍

Recommended by Cat Nelson

"Led by South Korean chef Bina Yu, who trained under Jean-Georges Vongerichten, the kitchen at Together seems to have it really... well... together. I go here for the octopus leg coated in *gochujang* and the grilled salmon brushed with an ume miso glaze. The atmosphere's polished but not uptight, a balance that often seems surprisingly hard for Shanghai to nail"—*CN*

Building 10, 546 Yuyuan Lu 愚园路546号10幢
+86 (0)21 5299 8928
Monday-Friday 11am-2pm and 6pm-10pm, Saturday 11.30am-2.30pm and 6pm-10pm, Sunday 11.30am-2.30pm • ¥¥¥¥

63 Bird

Recommended by Alex Xu, Jamie Barys

"A fun, modern restaurant with great wines that serves creative small plates. Lobin, who runs the wine side, always has a few hidden gems he's excited about, so ask him what he's got up his sleeve. Bird is also great if you're not a huge wine geek, as the staff are super-friendly and happy to guide you"—*AX*

"This natural wine bar serves by the half bottle, at the right price, so vino lovers can mix and match with their dinner (which is also excellent)"—*JB*

50 Wuyuan Lu 五原路50号 • +86 135 0172 6412
Wednesday–Monday 6pm–late (last orders 10.30pm), closed Tuesday
¥¥¥

64 Wu Guan Tang *Wu Guan Tang Su Shi* 五观堂素食

Recommended by Jenny Gao

"My favourite vegetarian restaurant in the city, a pretty lane house run by Buddhist monks. The space is serene and the hidden roof-top patio is a gem. The menu is a beautiful book, hand-written, full of inventive, seasonal dishes; you won't find mock meat in brown sauce here. Get the baked scalloped potato (烤土豆): under a golden caramelised top, it's pure butteriness. My other favourite is 'dragon eye beans' stir-fried in preserved olive leaves and served with *wowotou* (窝窝头), fluffy little concave *baos* of yellow cornmeal"—*JG*

349 Xinhua Lu 新华路349号
+86 (0)21 6281 3695 • *Open daily 11.30am–2.30pm and 3.30pm–9pm*
¥¥

65 Oriental House *Zui Dong* 醉东

Recommended by Xiaoyi Liu

"The owner here, Bei Ping, is originally from Taizhou, a small fishing village. He used to work in the fashion industry and had a dream of bringing Taizhou food to Shanghai. He worked with a chef to develop modern interpretations of the traditional dishes, including crispy intestine (脆皮大肠), claypot rice and yellow croaker, alongside a series of fusion dishes and craft cocktails"—*XL*

Room 202, 308 Anfu Lu 安福路308号202室
+86 (0)21 5410 7178
Open daily 11am–2pm and 5pm–12am
¥¥¥

66 Wan Party *Wan Hui* 皖荟

Recommended by Cat Nelson

"Mall dining is a bummer, but that's just a fact of life in this city (and country). Despite being one of China's eight great cuisines, the food of Anhui gets a hard time, probably due to its signature dish: fermented stinky fish. Wan Party is one of the few Anhui joints in Shanghai which makes it truly special, as does its 'tofu research centre'"—*CN*

No. 21ab 6F, Raffles City, 1193 Changning Lu
长宁路1193号(来福士广场东区6层21ab号)
+86 (0)21 6219 6113 • *Open daily 11am–2pm and 5pm–10pm*
¥¥¥¥

67 Oha

Recommended by Jamie Barys, Wei Diao, Cat Nelson

"Oha is an open kitchen with only 22 seats, inspired by Guizhou cuisine. The food is experimental and adventurous, using both Chinese and Western cooking techniques with Guizhou ingredients freshly flown in from the mountains. All the wines are natural, organic, bio-dynamic and rare. Usually it's booked up, especially at weekends, so make sure you make a reservation"—WD

"I think this place is a bit love-it-or-hate-it, as the kitchen can come on strong with its flavours (think pureéd century eggs), and I'm firmly in the love camp. Only a few spots really push the boundaries of what Chinese food can be, and this is one of them. Plus, it's got a super-intimate vibe and funky natural wines. You can get excellent coffee to go from the window outside, too"—CN

23 Anfu Lu, near Changshu Lu
徐汇区安福路23号，近常熟路
ohashanghai.com/project/
oha-eatery
+86 136 2164 7680
Open daily 11am–2pm and
5pm–10pm
¥¥¥

68 Kun Thai 堃泰

Recommended by Betty Richardson

"The only Thai restaurant in Shanghai worth going to, Kun Thai is run by a friendly Hong Kong boss who has somehow accumulated a kitchen of authentically Thai chefs. Don't expect thick green curries here, instead branch out and try the wonderfully herbal braised pork trotter (*khao ka moo*), clams in chilli sauce, supremely crunchy fried chicken thigh and fiery papaya salad with salted egg. The vibe is casual and affordable"—*BR*

Xinhua Century Park, 85 Yangzhai Lu 杨宅路85号新华世纪园底商
+86 136 4187 3965
Open daily 10.30am–10pm
¥¥¥¥

69 Okaeri

Recommended by Betty RIchardson

"An *izakaya*-style restaurant serving Taiwanese food to locals unwinding after work, Okaeri is perfect for low-key dining. It's equal parts restaurant and bar (stocked with a tempting selection of house-infused shochu and whisky), so you can order as much or as little as you want. I like the Taiwanese-style fried chicken, sausage with garlic, steamed clams with sake, and sesame oil chicken noodle soup. Note that the menu is only available in Chinese"—*BR*

B103, Lane 259 Jiashan Market, near Joanguo Xi Lu
嘉善路259弄B103, 近建国路
+86 139 1686 4639 • Open daily 6pm–1am • ¥¥¥¥

70 Lotus Eatery *Yun Zhi Yuan Yunnan Minzu Cai* 云之缘云南民族菜

Recommended by Cat Nelson

"They're gradually getting a bit more high-profile outside China now, but the flavours of Yunnan are surprising and radically different from what you might think of as 'Chinese food'. Lotus is a good introduction to the province's almost-south-east Asian dishes. It's our fall-back leaving-do location, because who wouldn't want their last memory to be pineapple rice and fried goat's cheese?"—*CN*

1112 Dingxi Lu 定西路1112号, 近武夷路 • +86 (0)21 6034 8168
Open daily 11.30am–10pm • ¥¥¥¥

71 Xime *Xi Mie* 嘻咩 ∡

Recommended by Michael Zee

"Hidden away around the back of a skyscraper is Xime, contemporary all-day Japanese cooking with some twists and turns to keep it fresh and exciting. If I'm there for lunch, I always add an order of deep-fried udon with curry dipping sauce to one of their excellent-value lunch sets, but if I'm there for dinner I'll try one of the new flavours of their house-infused sochus as a highball"—*MZ*

1-B, 1F, Century Business Plaza, 989 Changle Lu
长乐路989号世纪商贸广场1楼1-B
+86 (0)21 6422 5996 • *Open daily 11am–3pm and 5pm–11pm*
¥¥¥¥

WESTERN

Shanghai is where East eats West.

Purists may scoff at the thought of eating sourdough pizzas, avocado toast and artisanal hand-made burgers in China. They are wrong to do so. Shanghai has always been a city open to absorbing and consuming culinary influences from far and wide and the quality of many Western-style establishments goes above and beyond the expectations (and the stereotypes), to feed hungry locals and soothe homesick expats alike.

One of the most popular destinations for Western food is Found158 (158 Julu Lu), a submerged pit on the edge of the former French Concession (see page 6). Home to a wide selection of restaurants and bars, it has been hilariously dubbed 'foreigner park' (*lao wai gong yuan* 老外公园) and is a strange parody of the Chinatowns found elsewhere in the world.

The highlight of Found158 is Homeslice (see page 80), a New York-style pizzeria serving up 50cm pizzas as well as individual slices that will have Americans crying into their paper napkins. It's that good.

In Shanghai, many of the restaurants in this chapter would have been unimaginable a few years ago, but today, the world's flavours have been transported to this city, analysed and unpicked, restyled and reimagined, arguably better than the originals.

See also Highline and Gelato dal Cuore (pages 16 and 46).

72 Diner

Recommended by Michael Zee

"American comfort food. The portions here are very generous, so don't feel ashamed to share a plate of their Gold Standard pancakes topped with crushed Ferrero Rocher, or the disco fries finished with pork jowl, cheese and gremolata"—*MZ*

145 Wuyuan Lu 五原路145号
+86 (0)21 6416 1678
Sunday–Thursday 8am–10pm, Friday and Saturday 8am–12am
¥¥¥

73 Homeslice

Recommended by Michael Zee

"Homeslice is proof that an Englishman in China can make a better New York-style pizza than most Americans of Italian descent. The perfect sourdough crust – with toppings such as home-made ricotta and great local Sai Ua sausages made with the meat of heritage Chinese pigs – keep things more interesting than just pepperoni"—*MZ*

B1, 158 Julu Lu 巨鹿路158号158坊B1层
+86 (0)21 5309 9332
Sunday–Thursday 11am–12am, Friday and Saturday 11am–2am
¥¥¥¥

74 **Mercato**

Recommended by Alex Xu, Cat Nelson

"With great views and décor, this is the most consistently delicious and best value on the Bund. Many love the black truffle pizzas, but my go-to is the marinara (my wife is lactose intolerant). The perfectly seasoned tomato sauce allows the crispy chewy texture and yeasty flavour of the crust to shine in this minimalist pizza lover's dream. The menus change seasonally; I love house-made ricotta with strawberry jam, chargrilled octopus, salmon with porcini crust (ask for medium-rare), and crispy short rib. Pro tip: the swanky Jean-Georges on the fourth floor of the same building has a killer Friday night special: cocktails and egg caviar for 88RMB"—*AX*

"I'll be honest: I've only ever had pizzas at this gorgeous Italian spot by Jean-Georges Vongerichten on The Bund. They're all great, but the black truffle and farm egg pizza is how they made their name, and rightfully so, because it's off the hook. It accounts for 60 per cent of all the pizzas sold in the restaurant. You're in China, sure, but you really should eat a black truffle pizza here"—*CN*

6F, The Bund, 3 Zhongshan East Lu 中山东一路3号外滩三号6楼
mercato-international.com • +86 (0)21 6321 9922
Open daily 5.30pm–1am • ¥¥¥¥

75 **The Cannery**

Recommended by Cat Nelson, Wei Diao

"This is the kind of place you want in your neighbourhood and, even though it's not in mine, I find myself here with my dog for brunch on the terrace with an alarming frequency. There's an in-house fire pit (get the wood-plank salmon) and the gorgeous copper ceiling makes it a beautiful space to knock back some cocktails and oysters"—*CN*

"If I want to enjoy quality cocktails while indulging myself with protein, I go here. It is unconventional, but the brunch items are fairly familiar, with the low lounge seating that is always a plus. Also, it's not super-crowded, so you need have no worries about waiting in queues"—*WD*

Rm 106, Bldg 1, 1107 Yuyuan Lu, near Jiangsu Lu
愚园路1107号1号楼106室, 近江苏路
thecanneryshanghai.com
+86 (0)21 5276 0599
Monday–Friday 5.30pm–1am, Saturday and Sunday 11.30am–1am
¥¥¥¥

76 Villa Le Bec

Recommended by Wei Diao,
Betty Richardson, DJ Zhang

"A refuge for foie gras- and Burgundy-deprived French expats, endlessly glamorous Villa Le Bec has over the years established itself as Shanghai's most authentically Gallic dining destination. Its setting, a rambling renovated villa in the former French Concession, has helped, as there isn't a bad table in the house, nor the garden... nor the lamp-lit patio terrace for that matter. Chef-owner Nicolas Le Bec keeps the menu hearty but luxurious, with well-judged local inflections, such as the Chinese five spice-tinged duck breast. Must-orders include the creamy terrine de foie gras, or steak tartare, and, for a main course, a generous plate of black truffle pasta, or côte de boeuf with fabulous potato purée. Definitely save room for dessert, as you won't want to miss out on the zingy *tarte au citron*"—*BR*

"Run by chef Nicolas Le Bec and his wife Yu, this is a Shanghai institution. The food is impeccable (the black truffle pasta is a must-get) and best enjoyed with the meticulously curated wine list. Housed inside a villa with a bistro, private rooms and garden, it's a piece of France in Shanghai"—*DJZ*

321 Xinhua Lu 新华路321号
lebec.com.cn • +86 (0)21 6241 9100
Tuesday 6pm–late, Wednesday–
Sunday 12pm–late, Afternoon
tea Friday–Sunday 2pm–5pm,
closed Monday
¥¥¥¥

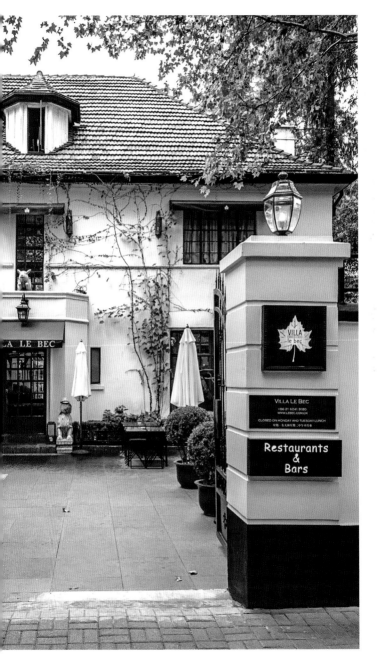

77 Commune Social

Recommended by Michael Zee

"Set in a former red-brick police station with a stripped-back industrial interior, the tapas-style menu draws influences from China, Spain and England. The real reason to visit is the dessert bar, headed by the lovely Kim Melvin, for something sweet made to order. It's a restaurant of pure charm and hospitable staff. Try brunch in the courtyard during the warmer months, too"—*MZ*

511 Jiangning Lu 江宁路511号
+86 (0)21 6047 7638
Tuesday–Sunday 11.30am–2.30pm, Tuesday–Thursday and Sunday 5.30pm–10pm, Friday and Saturday 5.30pm–10.30pm, closed Monday
¥¥¥

78 Raw

Recommended by Cat Nelson

"Raw's whole raison d'être is to serve top-flight ingredients with minimal intervention. Expect unfussy but thoughtful dishes – smoky dragon beans with garlic and chilli, or waygu-stuffed onions – often thrown in the Josper charcoal oven for just the right amount of char. It's the kind of place you come for a first date or a catch-up with friends: a relaxed and lively atmosphere, with exceptional but uncomplicated food"—*CN*

2/F, 98 Yanping Lu, near Xinzha Lu 延平路98号2楼, 近新闸路
+86 (0)21 5175 9818
Sunday and Tuesday–Thursday 5.30pm–12am, Friday and Saturday 5.30pm–1am, closed Monday • ¥¥¥¥

79 Pirata *Bi La Da* 比拉达

Recommended by Jamie Barys

"So much more than just Spanish, this late-night tapas joint pulls inspirations from the best of the Mediterranean, pillaging the culinary traditions of France, Italy and Greece among others. Run by a sea-worthy Taiwanese chef, the restaurant is a favourite among chefs, who come here after service for a taste of the juicy house-made chorizo"—*JB*

105A, Building 6, Columbia Circle, 1262 Yan'an Xi Lu
延安西路1262号(上生新所6号楼泳池畔105-A单元)
+86 (0)21 6117 2663
Open daily 6pm–12am • ¥¥¥

80 RAC Bar

Recommended by Camden Hauge, Cat Nelson, Alex Xu

"My go-to day-off dinner spot: a lovely courtyard, natural wines, great casual plates that are vaguely 'French' but are really just food you want to eat"—*CH*

"Weekends see it packed out with young, hip locals brunching on excellent Breton galettes, breakfast sandwiches, avocado toast and natural wines"—*CN*

"In the evening the space evolves into a wine bistro. The list is mainly trendy natural and orange wines with a few classic gems. My go-to is Jacques Lassaigne's Le Vigne de Montgueux Blanc de Blancs"—*AX*

Building 1, 322 Anfu Lu, near Wukang Lu 安福路322号1幢, 近武康路
Sunday–Wednesday 8am–6pm, Thursday–Saturday 8am–11pm • ¥¥¥¥

High-end dining in Shanghai can offer experiences that you won't find anywhere else in the world, as the city is rapidly finding and defining its own character and voice in food.

At Ultraviolet (see page 88), restaurant meets theatrical spectacle. The restaurant is pioneering the use of augmented reality and its immersive projections are where your dinner meets a dizzying, *Bladerunner*-like future.

Whether you're eating at a restaurant along the Bund – with a view of the iconic Lujiazui skyline, the envy of many other cities around the world – or feasting on dishes filled with ingredients such as dried abalone or luxury imported beef, which fetch eye-watering prices for only marginally more flavour than their cheaper counterparts, it can be easy to spend a lot of money in Shanghai.

But special shouldn't mean expensive and, in this city, it doesn't have to.

Thankfully, there is a renewed appreciation for the spirit of the traditional eight regional styles of Chinese cookery, along with Buddhist traditions of vegetarian and veganism. This respect for the way things have always been done can be seen at restaurants such as Yu Zhi Lan, Wujie and Fu He Hui (see right, pages 92 and 93). These restaurants are continuing the evolution of fine Chinese cuisine without inflicting significant harm on your bank balance.

Obviously any one of the restaurants in this chapter is a hot ticket, so reservations are essential.

See also Villa Le Bec (page 82).

81 Yu Zhi Lan 玉芝兰

Recommended by Betty Richardson

"What better way to acquaint yourself with Chinese fine dining and Sichuan food? Set in a stunning renovated villa in the former French Concession, this Chengdu export serves set menus that take your tastebuds on a whirlwind tour through the extraordinary variety of flavours in Sichuanese cooking, ranging from multi-coloured noodles to enormous chilli oil-soused dumplings. The chef insists on laborious methods that have all but disappeared from most restaurant kitchens, and is fanatical about sourcing the best raw ingredients China has to offer. A treat for the senses"—*BR*

851 Julu Lu 巨鹿路851号 • +86 (0)21 5466 5107
Open daily 10.30am–2pm and 5pm–10.30pm • ¥¥¥¥

82 Ultraviolet

Recommended by Jamie Barys

"Shanghai's hottest ticket is one of the 10 seats at the table of this 'full sensory dining experience'. The tongue-in-cheek haute cuisine menu serves 20 courses that deliver 'psycho-taste' by pairing each dish with a drink, as well as a sound, a visual projection and – sometimes – a scent. Tables book out three months in advance"—*JB*

uvbypp.cc; online bookings only
Tuesday–Saturday 6.30pm (one sitting), closed Sunday and Monday
¥¥¥¥

83 PHÉNIX at the PuLi 斐霓丝

Recommended by Wei Diao, Michael Zee

"Even the items on the breakfast buffet are carefully selected. It's worth knowing this place also does a good Sunday brunch"—*WD*

"The star is the duck neck sausage... just get it. (With the head attached in all its glory.) The neck is stuffed with foie gras and pork; total Chinese gore, but exquisite fun. The unique wine menu includes many bottles from China"—*MZ*

2nd Floor, PuLi Hotel, 1 Changde Lu 常德路1号璞丽酒店2楼
thepuli.com • +86 (0)21 2216 6988 • Open daily 6.30am–10.30am,
12pm–2.30pm and 6pm–10pm; Sunday brunch 11.30am–2.30pm
¥¥¥¥

84 Yong Yi Ting

Recommended by Cat Nelson

"It's off the beaten track for many, as the Mandarin Oriental is tucked in a quiet area of Pudong, but the Chinese restaurant here is worth travelling for. Tony Lu, arguably one of the country's most talented chefs, presents incredibly sophisticated Shanghainese and Jiangnan cuisine, such as delicate Taihu Lake shrimp and a supremely crispy Mandarin fish with sweet and sour sauce"—*CN*

LG, Mandarin Oriental Pudong Shanghai, 111 Pudong Nan Lu
浦东南路111号文华东方酒店LG层 • mandarinoriental.com/shanghai
+86 (0)21 2082 9978
Open daily 11.30am–2.30pm and 5.30pm–10.30pm
¥¥¥¥

85 Canton Table

Recommended by Cat Nelson

"What's better than *hargow*? Fried *hargow*. Canton Table's take on the shrimp dumpling standard is just one of its delightful modern renditions of dim sum classics. Just as stunning is the gorgeous dining room with views out to the Pudong skyline, making it quite the treat for lunch or brunch"—*CN*

5/F, 3 on the Bund, 3 Zhongshan Dong Yi Lu
threeonthebund.com/dining • +86 (0)21 6321 3737
Monday–Friday 11.30am–2.30pm, Saturday and Sunday 11.30am–3pm,
Monday–Sunday 5.30pm–11.30pm
¥¥¥¥

86 Seventh Son *Jia Quan Qi Fu* 家全七福

Recommended by Camden Hauge, Michael Zee

"Some of the best dim sum in Shanghai. They also do a great brunch"—*CH*

"For when you fancy splurging on top-notch Cantonese food, but not on a flight to Hong Kong. The must-order is the pineapple bun filled with *char siu* pork, it's a revelation! The egg yolk steamed buns should be left for a minute to cool (unless you like second-degree burns) and are not available on weekdays"—*MZ*

Tower 1, Room E2-03, 2F, Kerry Center, 1515 West Nanjing Lu
南京西路1515号嘉里中心一期二楼E2-03室
seventhson.hk • +86 (0)21 6266 3969 • Monday–Friday 11.30am–2.15pm,
Saturday and Sunday 11.30am–3pm, Monday–Sunday 5pm–10pm • ¥¥¥

87 **Bo Shanghai** *Chu Mo* 厨魔

Recommended by Cat Nelson

"Alvin Leung's speakeasy-style, contemporary fine dining Chinese restaurant ticks all the boxes for me. It's intimate without being stifling and the menu is challenging, provocative and unique. Working with the flavours of China's regional cuisine, the menu kicks off with Leung's signature molecular *xiaolongbao*. I'm still thinking about the duck kidney confit with pickled duck tongue, Sichuan peppercorn and lavender jelly I ate there two years ago!"—*CN*

6F, 5 The Bund, 20 Guangdong Lu 广东路20号外滩五号6楼
+86 (0)21 5383 3656 • Tuesday–Sunday 6.30pm–11pm, closed Monday
¥¥¥¥

88 **Wujie** *Da Shu Wu Jie* 大蔬无界

Recommended by Cat Nelson

"I'm constantly seeking out modern Chinese cuisine and this vegetarian restaurant consistently impresses. In a sense, it's fusion cooking, as dishes draw on a spectrum of flavours and techniques. But, at its core, the kitchen is forging a new path for contemporary Chinese food, and they've won a Michelin star for it"—*CN*

4F, 22 The Bund, Zhongshan East Second Lu
中山东二路外滩22号4楼
+86 (0)21 6375 2818
Open daily 11am–10.30pm
¥¥¥¥

89 Fu He Hui 福和慧

Recommended by Xiaoyi Liu, Wei Diao, Michael Zee

"Delights from Ningbo. Don't miss the pork lard and taro stew (looks terrible, tastes delicious), fried tile fish, or steamed butterfish. And finish with the famous Ningbo rice dumpling with black sesame filling!"—*XL*

"A historical building with nice greenery, excellent service and tasty food"—*WD*

"Both vegetarians and meat eaters will leave completely joyous. Try the beautiful tea pairing served in china from Spin Ceramics (see page 129) and ask about the off-menu items. A true vegetable-centric fine dining gem"—*MZ*

1037 Yuyuan Lu 愚园路1037号 • +86 (0)21 3980 9188
Open daily 11am–2pm and 5.30pm–11pm • ¥¥¥¥

COFFEE

The Chinese are relative newcomers to coffee drinking but, within the next decade, China is set to become the largest consumer of coffee in the world, overtaking America. Shanghai is leading the trend and the changes that happen there within the next 10 years will have a huge impact on the global coffee market.

With little-to-no traditional coffee-drinking culture, the Shanghainese have felt free to go in at the high end. Xuhui district is where you find many of the independent coffee shops. % Arabica (see page 99) commands enormous queues at weekends and serves third wave Japanese-style coffee, while local favourites such as Rumors and Shanghailander (see pages 97 and 98) offer a more relaxed vibe.

China is also a coffee-producing country, with most of the crop coming from Yunnan in the south. The harvest is relatively small, compared to countries such as Brazil, and the majority is drunk domestically. Try it at SeeSaw (see page 96) as a 'pour over', to enjoy the honey and floral flavours.

Luckily for tourists, it's rare for a coffee shop in Shanghai not to have fluent English-speaking staff and a menu in English, too (sometimes there isn't even Chinese!) but, if you feel some guilt, here are the names of the most common coffees.

- Cappuccino *Ka Bu Qi Nuo* 卡布奇诺
- Flat White *Ao Bai* 奥白
- Latte *Na Tie* 拿铁
- Americano *Mei Shi Ka Fei* 美式
- Espresso *Nong Suo* 浓缩
- Mocha *Mo Ka* 摩卡

See also Egg, Luneurs Boulanger + Glacier, Pain Chaud, Oha and RAC Bar (see pages 15, 43, 45, 74 and 85).

90 Bitter

Recommended by Camden Hauge

"I'm a bit biased, what with having two of my own cafés! At Bitter, I take our house pour, a 'Short Bitter' (similar to a cortado), with oat milk. We use custom roasted and blended beans from local streetwear and café brand DOE"—*CH*

58 Wuyuan Lu, near Changshu Lu
五原路58号, 近常熟路
+86 135 0172 6412
Wednesday–Monday 8am–late, Tuesday 8am–5pm
¥¥¥¥

91 SeeSaw

Recommended by Michael Zee

"Shanghai born-and-raised SeeSaw coffee set the bar high when they opened in 2012. Their cafés and branding are the epitome of cool, the coffee of exceptional quality, and they work directly with farms around the world to source their beans. Their honey-washed Yunnan beans also make a lovely gift"—MZ

Various branches, including 102, Building 19, Columbia Circle, 1262 Yun'an Xi Lu
延安西路1262号19号楼102(上生新所)
seesawcoffee.com • +86 (0)21 5258 7710
Open daily 10am–8pm • ¥¥¥¥

92 Rumors

Recommended by Wei Diao

"Rumors offers various drip coffee selections, using high-quality beans"—*WD*

While the trend in Shanghai seems to be that every new coffee shop has to be just achingly cool, Rumors is like an old comfortable pair of shoes. It's unpretentious in its attitude, serving mainly 'pour over' coffees from all around the world.

9A Hunan Lu
湖南路9甲
+86 (0)21 3460 5708
Open daily 11am–7.30pm
¥¥¥¥

93 Moon Coffee Roasters *Yue Giu Ka Fei* 月球咖啡

Recommended by Xiaoyi Liu

"One of the pioneers of the local third-wave speciality coffee trend, this place was started years ago and is still alive! They roast their own beans, with rare small-batch single-origin coffee available, such as 'Geisha Village'. On the expensive side, but definitely worth visiting for hard-core coffee addicts"—*XL*

2-2, 75 Maoming North Lu
茂名北路75弄2-2
+86 175 2104 5166
Open daily 10am–10pm
¥¥¥¥

94 Uncle No Name Espresso

Recommended by Michael Zee

"This is my local coffee shop. The coffee is superb, but my favourite drink here is the espresso and tonic water… sounds bizarre, but I drink one several times a week. Upstairs all the seats have power outlets and USB ports, so you can work here all day if you want to, while looking out to one of Shanghai's most photogenic roads"—*MZ*

178 Yongkang Lu
永康路178号
+86 (0)21 5456 6308
Open daily 8am–7pm
¥¥¥¥

95 Shanghailander (Coffee Bar) *Ju Fu* 聚福

Recommended by Michael Zee

"Wonderful coffee, excellent pastries and a bonus of flamboyant floral displays. Sometimes the owner, Daniel, will play something on the piano, too. What I like most about the Shanghailander is the attention to detail: the ceramics are all hand-made in Jingdezhen, the staff remember who you are… it's one of the most charming and personable coffee shops I know"—*MZ*

394 Wulumuqi South Lu
乌鲁木齐南路394号
Monday–Friday 8am–8pm, Saturday and Sunday 9am–6pm
¥¥¥¥

96 % Arabica Shanghai Roastery

Recommended by Betty Richardson

"Although it is an export rather than a proudly made-in-Shanghai concept, % Arabica has a few benefits that make it one of my favourites. The first is the quality of the coffee itself (as good as anything you'll find back home) and the second is its convenient proximity to Shanghai's famous Bund. Come the weekend, few things remind me why I love Shanghai more than strolling, coffee in hand, along the waterfront, taking in the architecture" —BR

1F, Xiejin Building, 169 Yuanmingyuan Lu
圆明园路169号协进大楼一楼
arabica.coffee • +86 153 0085 8178
Monday–Thursday 8am–8pm, Friday–Sunday 8am–9pm • ¥¥¥¥

TEA

Tea is the embodiment of ancient Chinese craft and tradition, from the manufacturing of porcelain, to the poetry and ceremony surrounding how to drink it. Whether you're drinking a matcha in Japan, a chai in India or a milky builder's in England, all tea originates from China. The diversity of styles, techniques and terroir means that, while tea remains the drink of the masses, the top end stuff can often sell for more than its weight in gold.

In many restaurants, green tea (*tieguanyin* 龙井 铁观音) is commonly served. Often this is complimentary and the pot will be topped up throughout the meal. Black tea in Chinese is called red tea (红茶), because of the colour of the drink, whereas the English name comes from the colour of the leaf. With the exception of pu'er (普洱茶), a fermented tea pressed into solid blocks, only ever buy loose-leaf tea.

For centuries, tea drinking was the antithesis of a fast-paced world, until about five years ago when the entire market changed. Now China is in a new tea craze. Brands such as HeyTea (see right) have reinvigorated sales and command queues of up to six hours for cream cheese-capped tea. It has a captive market of local teenagers and is worth a try, even just the once. Here are some tea varieties you may encounter:

- White tea 白茶 – *Bai Mudan* 白牡丹, *Baihao Yinzhen* 白毫银针

- Green tea 绿茶 – *Anji Bai Cha* 安吉白茶, *Baimao Hou* 白毛猴, *Biluochun* 碧螺春, *Huangshan Maofeng* 黄山毛峰, *Long Jing Cha* 龙井茶

- Oolong tea 乌龙茶 – *Tie Guan Yin* 铁观音, *Rougui* 肉桂, *Shui Xian* 水仙, *Da Hong Pao* 大红袍

- Black tea 红茶 – *Keemun* 祁门红茶, *Lapsang Souchong* 立山小种, *Yingdehong* 英德红茶, *Dianhong* 滇红

See also Laoximen Tea Market (page 129).

97 HeyTea *Xi Cha* 喜茶

Recommended by Camden Hauge, Michael Zee

"HeyTea totally deserves its hype. I couldn't understand the mania for the puréed fruit or fruit teas capped with a salted cheese cream... until I tried it" —CH

Various branches, including Sun Moonlight Center Plaza, 618 Xujiahui Lu (opposite Taikang Food Market)

徐家汇路618号日月光中心广场泰康区 泰康菜场对面
heytea.com • +86 (0)21 5410 6320
Monday–Thursday and Sunday 10am–10pm, Friday and Saturday 10am–10.30pm • ¥¥¥¥

98 Gui Pu Cha Kongjian 归朴茶空间

Recommended by Michael Zee

"Down a residential lane, through a discreet doorway, you'll find a rather beautiful small tea shop. Gui Pu means 'to return home'... and here you'll feel like you're sipping tea in someone else's house, which is nearly the same thing. Order a few small plates of cake and fruit to snack on as you work your way through the teas on offer, otherwise you'll end up tea-drunk"—*MZ*

1F, No. 12, 619 Jianguo West Lu
建国西路619弄12号1楼
+86 159 2162 1572
by appointment only, telephone for a reservation
¥¥¥¥

99 Fan Ji Keting 梵几客厅

Recommended by Wei Diao

"A great venue hidden behind the famous Wukang Lu, where there are far fewer people milling around. They don't like publicity at Fan Ji Keting, as it goes against the vibe of what they are doing here, so you'll have to go looking for the place. It has a modern Chinese interior design with fine furniture. Teaware is carefully selected and customised for the space. It is really worth seeking out"—*WD*

370 Wukang Lu
武康路370号
¥¥¥¥

100 Wanling Tea House *Wan Ling Cha Yuan* 婉玲茶苑

Recommended by Jamie Barys

"The daughter of Fujianese tea farmers, owner Wanling hosts educational classes and tea ceremonies in both English and Chinese languages. Her knowledge of tea is unparallelled and her passion, although zen-like, is palpable. She also sells tea leaves and beautiful teaware, which all come with stories about the producers"—*JB*

No 1, 619 Jianguo West Lu
建国西路619弄1号
wanlingteahouse.com • +86 (0)21 6054 0246
by appointment only, email or telephone for a reservation
¥¥¥¥

101 Xin Yuan 馨元

Recommended by Michael Zee

"During the day, Xin Yuan is like any other casual, contemporary tea shop, with Japanese-influenced interiors and – the centrepiece – an enormous light in the shape of the moon that dominates the space. Come dusk, it transforms into an elegant cocktail bar, with a drinks menu drawing on the long list of teas for infusions and other creative libations"—*MZ*

127 Wuxing Lu
吴兴路27号
+86 (0)21 5456 6618
Open daily 10am–1am
¥¥¥¥

102 YinXi Tea House *Yin Xi Cha Guan* 隐溪茶馆

Recommended by Michael Zee

"YinXi is where a traditional tea house, separate from the rhythm of the hustle and bustle outside, meets the modern world. You can hire a contemporary glass pod floating on a pond that seats about six people for a private event, sample lapsang souchong made with bamboo water from Anji in a Japanese tatami-lined room, or sip on oolong from Wuyi in a European-style drawing room. There is something for everyone"—*MZ*

750 Zhaojiabang Lu
肇嘉浜路750号
+86 (0)21 6466 0817
by appointment only, telephone for a reservation
¥¥¥¥

103 InWe 因味茶

Recommended by Michael Zee

"InWe is part of the new wave of tea drinking in China. In contrast to the lengthy tea ceremonies of yore, InWe is a reflection of a sleek and sexy Shanghai. The name is a play on *yin wei cha* (因为茶), which means 'because of tea', and the menu lists 'tea with ideas' such as a sparkling plum pu'er with enzymes or – for the adventurous – a white tea with Chinese olives. In a country that is slowly becoming hooked on coffee, here an ancient tradition takes a step forward"—*MZ*

Unit 115-116, Westgate Mall, 1038 Nanjing West Lu (entrance on Jiangning Lu)
南京西路1038号梅龙镇广场115-116室
+86(0)21 6271 6832
Monday–Friday 7.30am–10pm, Saturday and Sunday 10am–10pm
¥¥¥¥

COCKTAILS

It's inconceivable that in a city with so many skyscrapers, rooftops and mysterious hidden alleyways, there won't be a late-night tipple or two to be found.

Shanghai has its fair share of gimmicky speakeasies, hiding behind a fake façade for a launderette or hairdresser. But – as with all speak-easy bars around the world – they are often more style than substance. If you're looking for a reliable and uncomplicated bar, or something flashy that's still able to turn out perfect versions of the classics, you couldn't be in a better city. Entertainingly, the Chinese for 'cocktail' is a direct translation from the English: *ji wei jiu* (鸡尾酒), which literally means 'chicken tail drink'.

For a chic all-day option, neighbourhood locals such as Bitter (see page 95) cater for liquid lunchers and make a cracking Ayi-tini, made by their former *ayi* now turned famous cocktail maestro (find the recipe on page 137).

But you're in Shanghai to try something uniquely Chinese, aren't you? Perhaps something made with *baijiu* (白酒). Distilled from either rice, wheat or sorghum (or a mixture), it is split into four main styles: rice aroma (米香); light aroma (清香); sauce aroma (酱香); and strong aroma (浓香). Often of incredible strength, it puts the punchiest whisky to shame.

Try the Wolfberry-tini at tiny hidden gem Magpie (see page 112) for your *baijiu* fix, or check out City'Super (see page 125) to buy a bottle to take home.

See also Highline, Oha, Bitter and Xin Yuan (pages 16, 74, 95 and 105).

104 Senator Saloon

Recommended by Jenny Gao

"I hate to promote a place that doesn't need any more publicity, but I've spent more time in Senator Saloon than anywhere else in Shanghai. The very potent old-fashioned is the best bang for your buck, but also the most consistently perfect I've had anywhere, full-stop. Don't sleep on the food, either. You can't beat the cheesy edamame, pork belly sliders or mac 'n' cheese for soaking up the alcohol when you're in too far" —JG

98 Wuyuan Lu 五原路98号
senatorsaloon.com • +86 (0)21 5423 1330
Open daily 5pm–late • ¥¥¥¥

105 Bar No. 3

Recommended by Wei Diao, Michael Zee

"This place embodies the seasonal, simple, ingredient-driven style of craft cocktails, and house riffs on classics, using home-made liqueurs or syrups. The buzzing and cosy vibe is suitable for romance or a gathering of friends"—*WD*

"The extensive, evolving cocktail menu is full of clever puns and delightful flavours. I am grateful that the employee noodles are always on the menu. They remind me somehow of a Chinese twist on a bolognese and, after three or four cocktails, are just what you need"—*MZ*

277 Xingguo Lu 兴国路277号 • *ohashanghai.com/project/bar-no-3*
+86 (0)21 6418 2877 • Open daily 11am–2am • ¥¥¥¥

106 Blackbird

Recommended by Wei Diao

"Both the building and the interior are a showcase of cool design. Cocktails here are key, using clarified juices and more unusual ingredients. The outside space makes you feel as if you are on holiday and it has a nice terrace with the garden plants, rare herbs and spices that supply the restaurant"—*WD*

Columbia Circle, Building 8, 1262 Yan'an West Lu
延安西路1262号8号楼
+86 187 0199 0479
Open daily 11am–2am
¥¥¥¥

107 Avenue Joffre

Recommended by Wei Diao, Michael Zee

"A place where you will get very good service and high-quality drinks and – importantly – where you can always get a cosy seat"—*WD*

"Avenue Joffre has the unique ability to transport you to somewhere else. For locals, after a few sips of a Joffre Tea or Francis Alberta – along with the famed hospitality of Mune-san – you can close your eyes and imagine yourself in some hidden gem of a bar in Tokyo"—*MZ*

1F, Building 5, Yongjiating, 570 Yongjia Lu 永嘉路570号永嘉庭5号楼1楼
+86 (0)21 6029 9725 • Open daily 7pm–3am
¥¥¥¥

108 Epic

Recommended by Cat Nelson

"An understated cocktail bar set over several floors of narrow lane house in the former French Concession. Epic turns out impressive drinks without the pretention. The spirited bartender Cross Yu is full of wacky, fun ideas – for instance, serving a cocktail in a meringue, or in a sprinkle-coated glass – and the execution is perfect"—*CN*

17 Gaoyou Lu 高邮路17号
+86 (0)21 5411 1189
Open daily 6pm–late
¥¥¥¥

109 Shake

Recommended by Cat Nelson

"This sassy supperclub has it all. Live funk and soul performances most nights, solid Asian-inspired eats and excellent cocktails. The drinks are as strong and captivating as the vibes here. Shake's my go-to with out-of-town guests, or for when I want something different from just a standard evening of hitting the bars with friends and colleagues"—CN

3/F, 46 Maoming South Lu
茂名南路46号3楼
shakeclub.cn • +86 (0)21 6230 7175
Tuesday–Sunday 6pm–2am, closed Monday
¥¥¥¥

110 Magpie Cocktail Bar 2 *Xi Que* 喜鹊

Recommended by Michael Zee

"A pocket-sized cocktail bar in the former French Concession. The entire bar is lit with red lamps, so you don't look at all drunk in that selfie. Absolutely try the Wolfberry-tini. If you're at all musically inclined, they also have a wide selection of instruments available – from guitars to Tibetan singing bowls – that you can pick up and play. If not, don't worry, the owner and many of the clientele will serenade the night away for you"—MZ

42 Wanping Lu
宛平路42号
+86 150 0036 5905
Monday–Thursday 6pm–1am, Friday 5pm–2am, Saturday 3pm–2am, Sunday 1pm–11pm
¥¥¥¥

111 Union Trading Company

Recommended by Camden Hauge, DJ Zhang, Jamie Barys

"Edgy, elegant drinks in a locals-only environment. Yao, the owner, keeps the vibe friendly and down-to-earth, with excellent service" —CH

'Mean cocktails and fat-tastic American food, such as burgers, fried chicken enders with Sichuan spice and 'tachos' (tater tots with nacho toppings)" —DJZ

judge a bar as much by its snack menu as its drink list. Union nails both. The urger is in a class of its own, as is the Waltzing Matilda cocktail" —JB

!o 2, 64 Fenyang Lu 汾阳路64弄2号 • +86 (0)21 6418 3077

,Monday–Saturday 6pm–2am, closed Sunday • ¥¥¥¥

WINE

Long before the rise of China's middle class, foreign and imported wines were regarded as status symbols. Red wine is still more popular than white wine today, because the colour represents good luck in Chinese culture.

Modern tastes have shifted away from domestic *baijiu* (see page 108) and continue to diversify. On menus, bold French reds appear alongside natural, skin contact and biodynamic wines from the New World and those from Chinese growers who are part of the New Latitude style of wineries.

Unless you're a serious wine buff, you'll probably never have tried (or even heard of) wines from Ningxia, Xinjiang or Yunnan, all westerly provinces with greatly differing climates, from desert to mountains. Ningxia, often referred to as 'Chinese Napa', is home to more than 100 wineries. You can try wine from Kanaan winery at PHÉNIX (see page 90) or at bars such as Vinism (see page 118), which offer a constantly evolving list you can sample by the glass.

Wine production and quality are increasing year on year in China, and you'll find award-winning Chinese wines (*pu tao jiu* 葡萄酒) in your local supermarket someday soon.

See also Bird, RAC Bar and City'Super (see pages 72, 85 and 125).

A note on beer (*pi jiu* 啤酒)

Whether it's a salty fish dish or a spicy hot pot, the bold flavours of Chinese food are often best paired with a beer. But Shanghai is not really a beer-drinking city. Of course there are plenty of bars, breweries and restaurants all serving Qingdao or Harbin. But, if you want somewhere full of character with interesting international and local beers, get on a train to Beijing.

112 Le Verre à Vin

Recommended by Alex Xu, Xiaoyi Liu

"A fun wine bar, with ceilings and walls covered with hand-written signs and drawings. There is a 'wall of wine' with prices written on the bottle, from the edgy and natural to the classic. Pro tip: Sushi Takumi, a six-seater *omakase* next door, is a hidden gem. Mention you are eating there and you can buy wine from the selection at Le Verre à Vin to enjoy with your sushi"—AX

"One of the first casual wine bistros in Shanghai. Affordable food, a great vibe (it reminds me of a Japanese *izakaya*) and two shelves of wine to choose from with a heavy focus on natural wine. Good for hangouts and parties"—XL

1221 Changle Lu 长乐路1221号 • +86 (0)21 5403 4278
Open daily 5.30pm–1am • ¥¥¥¥

113 Shanghailander Wine Café *San Nian Jian* 叁年间

Recommended by Alex Xu

"A great spot affiliated with wine education company Grapea, which puts on weekly events from intimate classes to comparative regional tastings. While the by-the-glass list can be limited, there is a great page of wines at the end, hand-picked by the owner, with back vintages and specialities such as the 2007 Gravner Bianco Breg I enjoyed recently. It is in a courtyard surrounded by a bakery, a pizza place and a skewer joint. On Sundays, I sit outside, order wine and bites from neighbouring restaurants and drink away the afternoon"—AX

1/F, Building 2, 692 Yongjia Lu 永嘉路692号2幢一楼
+86 (0)21 6403 0519 • Open daily 9am–10pm • ¥¥¥¥

114 No Name

Recommended by Michael Zee

"What this place lacks in size, it makes up for with heart. The staff are complete wine nerds and will wax lyrical with stories of the winemakers and the grapes they serve. No matter what your taste or budget, there will be a glass here for you"—MZ

564 Wanhangdu Lu
万航渡路564号
Open daily 4pm–12am
¥¥¥¥

115 Le Bec Boutique

Recommended by DJ Zhang, Xiaoyi Liu

"Villa Le Bec (see page 82) is known to be one of the best French restaurants in Shanghai. Just down the street is its wine bar and grocery store, stocked with a myriad of red, white and sparkling choices to wine-in or take home. The boutique is open all day and serves simpler dishes than its Villa counterpart, such as cold cuts and cheese, *croque monsieur*, beef stew and spaghetti bolognese, as well as a variety of baked goods"—*DJZ*

"Opened by the legendary Nicolas Le Bec, this shop-cum-wine bar has a very competitive selection of French fine wine, and only 100RMB corkage if you'd like to drink on site. My favourite place to go when I'm craving traditional French wine. Only downside: French wine only"—*XL*

62 Xinhua Lu
新华路62号
lebec.com.cn
+86 (0)21 6241 9100
Tuesday 4pm–10pm, Wednesday–Sunday 10am–10pm, closed Monday
¥¥¥¥

116 Vinism

Recommended by Wei Diao, Michael Zee

"The owner is obsessed with natural wines. Do not hesitate to ask for his recommendations"—WD

"Natural wine lovers rejoice! This is the perfect neighbourhood wine bar. It's on the same street as Xian Mo Rou Jia Mo and one block away from Old Style Ningbo (see pages 40 and 67) so, if you're pre- or post-dinner, their selection of wines will keep your night flowing, regardless of what day of the week it is"—MZ

57-1, Dongzhu'anbang Lu
东诸安浜路57-1号
+86 (0)21 3212 0759
Open daily, wine cellar 2pm–late, kitchen 5pm–11pm
¥¥¥¥

MARKETS & INGREDIENTS

Shanghai has a market for everything. Whether you're looking for pearls, sex toys, wine glasses, reading glasses, counterfeit luxury goods, hotel catering supplies, fresh flowers, fake flowers, silk fabric, pu'er tea, or just a few carrots, there will be a complex, building or warehouse with hundreds of vendors waiting for your custom.

Before the introduction of Western-style supermarkets and online shopping, the Shanghainese would go (and many still do) to buy their groceries from wet markets. 'Wet' because of the availability of live fish, crabs and other aquatic animals such as frogs and turtles. They are a one-stop shop for fruit, vegetables, dry groceries, fresh noodles and tofu and hand-made dumplings to enjoy in a hot pot at home. Some are small – meant only for the local community – and others enormous, with multiple floors and sections.

The most common unit of measurement in China is *yi jin* (一斤), which is equivalent to 500g, but you could also ask for *yi ba* (一把), which means 'a handful', or *yi dian dian* (一点点), 'a little bit'.

If you're looking for something from a faraway land, or some Western home comforts, you may have to go to a specialist. Within the expat community, there is no one more famous than the Avocado Lady (see page 125); one of the first people to sell avocados in Shanghai, she is also the purveyor of all sorts of delicious treats from around the world that larger supermarkets don't stock. If she doesn't have it in her tiny shop on Wulumuqi Lu, then be sure to ask and she will do her best to get it for you.

See also Yongnian Breakfast Market and Laoximen Tea Market (pages 18 and 129).

117 Jinhua Ham Guy on Wulumuqi Lu
Ju Feng Yan La Shangdian 聚凤腌腊商店

Recommended by Camden Hauge, Michael Zee

"The best stretch for home shopping, with Chinese Jinhua ham or Sichuan sausages here, the famed Avocado Lady, a wet market, great Lebanese dips and flatbread at Eli Falafel... and wine and beer from several bottle shops"—*CH*

"Ham from Jinhua is one of China's most prized ingredients. The hams look similar to Spanish varieties and the way they're made is largely the same. This guy is one of the cheeriest men in town, so ask lots of questions"—*MZ*

190 Wulumuqi Middle Lu 乌鲁木齐中路190号
+86 (0)21 6437 1608 • Open daily 7.30am–8pm • ¥¥¥

118 Fuxing Zhong Lu Wet Market
Fuzhong Cai Shichang
复中菜市场

Recommended by Michael Zee

"This is a gargantuan wet market. Set back from the road, the entire market is sectioned out. The ground floor as you enter is cooked meats, whole roasted ducks and bits of unidentifiable animals, with two ladies creating hand-made dumplings for home-made hot pot as well as raw *xiaolongbao*. The rest of the ground floor is primarily meat and – of course – live fish.

Upstairs there is one fruit guy, a lady selling eggs and about 30 vegetable stalls. I go to the husband-and-wife team opposite the watch and clock repairs, who have helped teach me what to do with every vegetable. At the back are several tofu, rice and dried goods stalls and, finally, a very small shop of imported goods. Within the entire spectrum of Chinese cuisine, there is almost nothing you cannot find here"—*MZ*

1239 Fuxing Middle Lu
复兴中路1239号
Open daily 6am–7pm
¥¥¥

119 Pudong Muslim Market
Pudong Qingzhensi Shaokao 浦东清真寺烧烤

Recommended by Jamie Barys

"Every Friday afternoon, the sidewalks around Pudong Mosque showcase culinary delights from the city's Muslim community. Think lamb in all its glorious forms, such as cumin lamb skewers with freshly baked naan and fried and oven-roasted mutton-stuffed dumplings. This food street is much cleaner (and less touristy) than its Puxi sister"—*JB*

375 Yuanshen Lu 源深路375号
Fridays only, 10am–3pm
¥¥¥¥

120 City'Super

Recommended by Betty Richardson

"For a homesick foreigner wandering through this enormous international supermarket, reacquainting oneself with the food and brand names from home can be a curiously emotional experience. Who knew you'd feel a pang at seeing all your favourite breakfast cereals again? Shopping here is certainly a step up in price from the local 'wet' markets, but the quality assurance of fresh ingredients (particularly meat, fish, eggs, fruit and vegetables) make City'Super an essential when shopping to cook at home"—BR

110-112, LG1, IAPM, 999 Huaihai Zhong Lu
淮海中路999号环贸广场LG1层110-112
citysuper.com.cn
+86 (0)21 5175 8208
Open daily 10am–11pm
¥¥¥¥

121 Avocado Lady *Hong Feng Fu Shipin Shangdian*
红峰副食品商店

Recommended by Wei Diao, Michael Zee

"This place provides imported ingredients and almost everything a foreigner needs for home cooking, within a store of just 25 square metres in the French Concession. It sells fresh ingredients at a fair price and will save the visitor time, when compared to big supermarkets in shopping malls"—WD

"As huge as Shanghai is, there are just some things the Chinese don't really have an appetite for. Enter the Avocado Lady! Her tiny shop has wonders such as fresh dill, heritage tomatoes and Marmite, which simply do not exist anywhere else in Shanghai. At weekends the shop is packed with expats from around the globe, but also curious locals who are purchasing a bottle of HP sauce for the first time, just to see what all the fuss is about"—MZ

274 Wulumuqi Lu
乌鲁木齐路274号
+86 (0)21 6437 7262
Open daily 6am–9pm
¥¥¥¥

PRESENTS

Gifting in China is an art form. Every occasion requires some ceremony, with elaborate packaging and decorative bags that often cost more than the present they carry.

If you receive a gift from a Chinese person, you might sense that it has had a previous owner. Unlike in the West, re-gifting is socially acceptable and widespread. The phrase *jie hua xian fo* (借花献佛) directly translates as 'borrowing flowers to give to Buddha' and, in many Chinese homes, there will be cupboards filled with presents awaiting their new owners... when the time is right.

For dried foods, there are several street-side markets around the Huaihai Lu and Xintiandi area, but one in particular that provides a wide choice is Bee Cheng Hiang (see page 129). Here you can pick up delightfully packaged snacks, or classic Shanghai candy such as White Rabbit.

A few years ago, it would have been common to glimpse a man at the side of the road hammering woks by hand, or stalls of husbands and wives bending bamboo into steamers of every size. Sadly they have all been cleared away by the local authorities, or have passed away.

Today, most locals – Chinese and expat – head to the Hotel Equipment Company, where you could buy all the hardware necessary to open your own Sichuan or Fujian restaurant. A wok will set you back about £5 depending on the size, but you can also find good-quality steamers, cleavers and just about anything else for the kitchen. You can find it online at hec.com.cn.

See also Egg and City'Super (pages 15 and 125).

122 Convenience Stores

Recommended by Cat Nelson, Michael Zee

"Honestly the best place for food gifts, no joke. They have served me well for a decade of in-a-pinch gifts before flying back home. The amount of whacky flavours of crisps alone is staggering" —*CN*

"I buy things from Lawson or FamilyMart as gifts and don't know what they are myself. Mystery is part of the fun. Ideal for Christmas stocking fillers" —*MZ*

Lawson • lawson.com.cn • Open daily 24 hours
FamilyMart • familymart.com.cn • Open daily 24 hours
7-Eleven • 7-11bj.com.cn • Open daily 7am–11pm
¥¥¥¥

123 Happy Clay *Shou Gong Taoci* 手工陶瓷

Recommended by Michael Zee

"Contemporary, colourful and one-off ceramic pieces, although sometimes it can be difficult to find two of the same thing. Located bang in the centre of town. This is where I go for gifts when I don't have the time to head out to Spin (see right)"—*MZ*

20 Donghu Lu 东湖路20号
happyclay.com
+86 (0)21 5404 8853
Open daily 12pm–9pm
¥¥¥¥

124 Laoximen Tea Market
Lao Xi Men Gu Wan Cha Cheng 老西门古玩茶城

Recommended by Jamie Barys

"There are tea shops on every street corner in Shanghai, but I prefer the wholesale tea markets where vendors are happy to pour you cup after cup, so you can try before you buy. Laoximen Tea Market is my pick for the friendliest sellers and I love the Tibetan tea shop on the second floor"—*JB*

1121 Fuxing East Lu 复兴东路1121号
+86 (0)21 5386 5555
Open daily 8am–9pm
¥¥¥¥

125 Spin Ceramics *Xuan* 旋

Recommended by Michael Zee, Camden Hauge

"The best place for stunning ceramics made in Jingdezhen, the spiritual home of porcelain in China. The showroom is huge, filled with timeless and chic designs. Something for everyone at an affordable price. Unfortunately, Spin has moved out of the city, though they're good enough to make an effort to get there. Call them for detailed directions, the staff speak fluent English"—*MZ*

"A hand-made tea set from Spin Ceramics is an amazing gift"—*CH*

F/1, Building D2, 5i Center II, 538 Hutai Zhi Lu
沪太支路538号飞马旅2期D2栋1层
spinceramics.com • +86 (0)21 6279 2545 • Open daily 11am–8pm • ¥¥¥¥

126 Bee Cheng Hiang *Mei Zheng Xiang* 美珍香

Recommended by Michael Zee

"A level up from getting gifts at Lawson or FamilyMart (see page 127), here food items come in fancier packaging, sometimes so fancy that the package costs more than its contents. They're most famous for their *bakkwa* (肉干), a cured meat from Fujian province that's popular across Asia and similar to jerky. Bee Cheng Hiang have expanded the range of flavours, so don't be afraid to ask for a tester"—*MZ*

Unit 5, 1/F, 988 Huaihai Middle Lu 淮海中路988号一楼05单元
beechenghiang.com.sg • +86 (0)21 5403 2629
Monday–Thursday 8am–9pm, Friday–Sunday 8am–9.30pm • ¥¥¥¥

RECIPES

Eight Treasure Porridge

Spring Onion Oil Noodles

Fresh Soy Milk

Shanghainese Braised Bran Dough

Sesame Noodles

Smashed Cucumber Salad

Shamisen Cocktail

Ayi-tini

Eight Treasure Porridge *Ba Bao Zhou* 八宝粥

This porridge has a myriad of health claims in traditional Chinese medicine. Originally it had eight ingredients, as you'd expect, but these days anything goes. It can be made with chicken stock and served with an evening meal, or with just water and sugar for a healthy and nutritious breakfast. It is traditionally cooked for the Laba Festival, which falls on the eighth day of the twelfth lunar month. You'll find all the ingredients available in Chinese supermarkets and grocers at home.

Serves 4

200g white rice

50g dried red beans

50g dried mung beans

50g unsalted peanuts

50g ginkgo nuts, shelled

50g pearl barley

50g lotus seeds

50g dried longan

5 Chinese red dates

Sugar, to taste

2 tbsp goji berries

2 tsp black sesame seeds

In 3 separate bowls, soak the white rice, red beans and mung beans in plentiful cold water. Leave overnight, or for at least 8 hours. Drain, discarding the water.

Put the drained red beans and mung beans and the peanuts in a saucepan with enough water to cover. Bring to a gentle simmer and cook for 20 minutes.

Add 750ml water to the pan along with the drained rice, ginkgo nuts, pearl barley, lotus seeds, longan and Chinese dates. Return to a gentle simmer and cook over a medium heat for a further 15–20 minutes, stirring often and splashing in just a little extra water if necessary.

Sweeten the porridge to taste and add the goji berries.

Take the pan off the heat and leave for 10 minutes, for the flavours to infuse. Serve sprinkled with black sesame seeds.

Spring Onion Oil Noodles *Cong You Mian* 葱油面

A staple noodle of Shanghai. The pungent oil dressing goes a long way and can be made in advance, ready to douse a portion of freshly cooked noodles for a quick lunch. Some restaurants, such as Dong Tai Xiang (see page 19), also add dried shrimps – which give an extra dimension of salty umami – but these are definitely optional if you want to keep it vegetarian (or even vegan, depending on the noodles you use).

Serves 4

4 tbsp flavourless cooking oil

12 spring onions, julienned

3 tbsp dark soy sauce

3 tbsp light soy sauce

2 tsp sugar

400g fresh Chinese noodles (or 250g dried noodles)

Heat the oil gently in a wok or frying pan.

Add the spring onions and cook gently for 3–4 minutes until they start to turn golden, fragrant and a little crisp. Remove half the onions and set aside.

Add the dark and light soy to the wok along with the sugar. Stir occasionally until the sugar has dissolved and the sauce is glossy.

Prepare the noodles according to the packet instructions, divide them between 4 bowls and equally pour the salty onion oil between them, or to taste (it can be a little overpowering).

Scatter with the rest of the crispy onions and serve immediately.

Fresh Soy Milk *Dou Jiang* 豆浆

This is the staple breakfast drink of millions of Chinese people. Freshly made, it doesn't even resemble the shelf-stable, gum-thickened horrors found in many Western supermarkets.

Serves 2
250g dried soy beans

Sugar, to taste

Cover the soy beans with water and leave to soak overnight, or for at least 8 hours. Drain, discarding the water, then wash the beans thoroughly.

Put the beans in a blender with 750ml water and blend until totally smooth. Pour through a fine-mesh sieve or muslin cloth into a saucepan.

Gently heat the milk for 8–10 minutes, but do not allow it to boil.

Add sugar to taste, allow to cool slightly, then serve.

Shanghainese Braised Bran Dough *Kao Fu* 烤麩

This is found on the menu of restaurants such as Jianguo328 (see page 64) as a topping on noodles. It is often served as a starter, either warm or at room temperature, but never hot from the wok or fridge-cold.

Serves 3–4

250g fresh bran dough (*kao fu*), or about 50g dried bran dough

Handful of dried wood ear mushrooms

Handful of dried day lily

Big handful of raw, skinned peanuts

Slug of flavourless vegetable oil

100g bamboo shoots, fresh or tinned

4 tbsp Chinese cooking wine, ideally Shaoxing

4 tbsp light soy sauce

2 tbsp dark soy sauce, or Shanghai braising soy sauce, if you can find it

2 tbsp sugar

2 spring onions, finely chopped

2 tbsp sesame oil

Big handful of edamame, podded (optional)

If using dried dough, first place it in a bowl with plenty of warm water and leave it for about 15 minutes to come back to life. Now discard the water and press as much of the liquid out as possible. Cut the dough into 2.5cm cubes.

Soak the wood ear mushrooms and day lily in 200ml freshly boiled water for 10 minutes. Drain, reserving the soaking water.

In a small saucepan, boil the peanuts for 10 minutes. Drain and set aside.

Heat the oil in a wok until very hot. Add the peanuts and stir for 30 seconds, then add the dough and stir for a further 2 minutes. Next, add the drained mushrooms and day lily, along with the bamboo shoots, and stir. Add the wine, light and dark soy sauces, sugar and reserved soaking water. Reduce the heat to low and cover.

Simmer for 45 minutes, checking every 15 minutes to make sure it hasn't boiled dry and splashing in a little water, if needed. Add the spring onions, sesame oil and edamame (if using) and stir through.

Decant into a bowl and leave until warm or at room temperature, then serve.

Sesame Noodles *Ma Jiang Mian* 麻酱面

This recipe is an adaptation of a dish from Wei Xiang Zhai (see page 29). There they use leftover oil from cooking pork chops and leftover sauce from braised pork to thin down the sesame sauce. Any leftover juices from a piece of roast meat will make this recipe a near-authentic recreation.

Chinese sesame paste is made from heavily toasted sesame seeds, whereas Middle Eastern tahini is made from untoasted sesame seeds and has a slightly bitter taste. At a pinch you can use tahini, but the Chinese variety is widely available, too, and preferable here.

Serves 2

2 tbsp Chinese sesame paste

1 tbsp smooth peanut butter

2 tbsp light soy sauce

2 tbsp black Chinese vinegar

100ml leftover hot meat juices, or boiling water

200g fresh Chinese egg noodles

2 spring onions, finely sliced

2 tsp chilli sauce or chilli oil, or to taste

In a bowl, combine the sesame paste, peanut butter, soy sauce, vinegar and meat juices (or boiling water) and stir gently until you have a smooth sauce.

Prepare the noodles according to the packet instructions and divide them between 2 bowls.

Top each bowl with half the sesame sauce and gently stir with chopsticks.

Sprinkle with the spring onions and chilli sauce or oil, to taste, then serve.

Smashed Cucumber Salad *Pai Huang Gua* 拍黄瓜

This salad is found on menus across the whole of China. It is served as a starter or an appetiser to many dishes from roast duck to dumplings. It is simple to prepare (and vegan).

Serves 2

3 garlic cloves, very finely chopped or finely grated

1 tbsp Chinese black vinegar

1 tbsp light soy sauce

1 tsp sesame oil

1 tsp sugar

Pinch of salt

1 large cucumber, or 3 smaller Persian cucumbers

In a small bowl, combine the garlic, vinegar, soy sauce, sesame oil, sugar and salt and set aside.

If you are using a large English-style cucumber, cut it open lengthways down the middle and remove half the watery seeds with a spoon.

Place a tea towel over the cucumber or cucumbers and – using a heavy cleaver or a saucepan – smash, so it is heavily bruised. Uncover and cut the cucumber into smaller bite-sized pieces.

When you're ready to serve, toss the cucumber in the dressing. Don't do this too far in advance.

Shamisen Cocktail

The famous and refreshing favourite from Bar No. 3 (see page 110), named after a traditional Japanese three-stringed instrument.

Makes 1

45ml single malt whisky

20ml apple liqueur

30ml vermouth blanc

1 tsp wild honey

1 lime wedge

2 lemon leaves, plus 1 to serve

Place all the ingredients in a cocktail shaker with a handful of ice cubes and shake for 15 seconds.

Double-strain into a coupe glass and garnish with a lemon leaf.

Ayi-tini

The ayi (auntie) at Bitter (see page 95) is something of a modern hero in China. From humble beginnings cleaning the bar, she was quickly promoted to bar manager, first making Shanghai's best martini and then (her own invention) the Ayi-tini.

Makes 1

90ml Citadelle gin

15ml dry vermouth

1 Buddha's Hand (a Chinese variety of lemon), or Meyer lemon

In a cocktail shaker with the largest ice block you can fit into it, combine the gin and vermouth and stir for 1 minute, or until the shaker is ice-cold to the touch.

Strain into a Nick and Nora glass.

Garnish with a pared strip of zest of Buddha's Hand or Meyer lemon and serve.

Glossary

Helpful phrases

I want this • 我要这个 • wǒ yào zhège
One portion • 一份 • yī fèn
Two portions • 两份 • liǎng fèn
Thank you • 谢谢 • xièxiè
I don't want it • 我不要 • wǒ bùyào
Hot • 热的 • rè de
Cold/iced • 冰的 • bīng de
It's too expensive! • 太贵了! • tài guìle!
To take away (like a coffee) • 带走 • dài zǒu
To take away/pack up food in a doggy bag • 打包 • dǎbāo
How much is this? • 多少钱? • duōshǎo qián?
Where is the toilet? • 洗手间在哪? • xǐshǒujiān zài nǎ?
Is it spicy? 这个辣妈? • zhège là mā?
I don't want spicy • 我不要辣 • wǒ bùyào là
I love spicy • 我爱辣 • wǒ ài là
I don't eat meat • 我不吃肉 • wǒ bù chī ròu
I'm a vegan • 我是纯素食者 • wǒ shì chún sùshí zhě
Can I get the bill? • 买单? • mǎidān?
What are your specials? • 你特色的菜是什么? • nǐ tèsè de cài shì shénme?
I want the same as him/her • 我想和他/她一样的食物 • wǒ xiǎng hé tā/tā yīyàng de shíwù
Delicious! • 好吃! • hǎo chī! OR *Very delicious!* • 非常美味! • feichǎng měiwèi!
Welcome • 欢迎光临 • huānyíng guānglín
Goodbye! • 拜拜! • bàibài!

Menus

MEAT
Ròu • 肉 • used alone means pork, but you will often see xiān ròu (鲜肉), which means 'fresh meat' for fresh pork or, in Muslim restaurants, mutton or lamb
Pork • 猪肉 • zhūròu
Beef • 牛肉 • niúròu
Fish • 鱼 • yú
Chicken • 鸡肉 • jīròu
Duck • 鸭肉 • yā ròu
Mutton • 羊肉 • yángròu
Offal – liver 肝 • gān; intestines • 肠 • cháng; lungs • 肺 • fèi

VEGETABLES AND CARBOHYDRATES
Tofu • 豆腐 • dòufu
Egg • 蛋 • dàn
Potato • 土豆 • tǔdòu
Aubergine • 茄子 • qiézi
Beans/peas • 豆 • dòu
Onions (and all alliums) • 葱 • cōng
Cucumber • 黄瓜 • huángguā
Pumpkin • 南瓜 • nánguā
Mushrooms • 蘑菇 • mógū
White rice • 白饭 • báifàn
Noodles • 面 • miàn
Bread • 面包 • miànbāo
Sesame • 芝麻 • zhima
Chilli/spicy • 辣 • là
Vegetables (this character is used for many green leafy vegetables) • 菜 • cài

HOME COOKING
Soy sauce • 酱油 • jiàngyóu
Shaoxing rice wine • 绍兴黄酒 • Shàoxīng huángjiǔ
Sesame oil • 香油 • xiāngyóu
Cooking oil • 食油 • shíyóu

COOKING STYLES
Wok-fried • 炒 • chāo
Braised • 烧 • shāo
Roasted/grilled • 烤 • kǎo
Chilled/served cold • 凉拌 • liángbàn
Sizzling in a metal pan • 干锅 • gān guō
Shredded/strips • 丝 • sī
Numbing spice (usually Sichuan food) • 麻辣 • má là

INDEX **A TO Z**

141

BLOOMSBURY PUBLISHING
Bloomsbury Publishing Plc
50 Bedford Square, London WC1B 3DP

BLOOMSBURY, BLOOMSBURY PUBLISHING and the Diana logo
are trademarks of Bloomsbury Publishing Plc

First published in Great Britain 2019

A catalogue record for this book is available from the British Library.

ISBN: 978 1 5266 0517 7

2 4 6 8 10 9 7 5 3 1

Series Editor: Lucy Bannell
Contributing Writer: Michael Zee
Cover Designer: Greg Heinimann
Typesetting: Phillip Beresford
Photographer: Betty Richardson
Production Controller: Gary Hayes

Printed and bound in India by Replika Press Pvt. Ltd

Bloomsbury Publishing Plc makes every effort to ensure that the papers used in the manufacture
of our books are natural, recyclable products made from wood grown in well-managed forests.
Our manufacturing processes conform to the environmental regulations of the country of origin.

To find out more about our authors and books visit
www.bloomsbury.com and sign up for our newsletters.

BREAKFAST & BRUNCH

1 Egg — E4
2 Highline — G4
3 Yongnian Breakfast Market — H5
4 Dong Tai Xian — G4
5 Mei Xin Dian Xin — G3
6 A Da Cong You Bing — G5
7 100 Nanyang Lu — E3
8 Xiao Tao Yuan — F5
9 Jianbing on Xiangyang Lu and Yongkang Lu — F5

XIAOLONGBAO

10 Man Long Chun — F5
11 Fahua Tangbao — C6
12 Lin Long Fang — H5
13 Fu Chun — D4
14 Shan Shan Xiaolongbao — D3
15 Wu You Xian — H8

NOODLES

16 Wei Xiang Zhai — G4
17 Gu Sha Wu Mian — G1
18 Liu Tang Men — C6
19 Cejerdary — B6
20 Yi Mian Chun Feng — D6
21 Lao Di Fang Mian Guan — F5
22 Henan La Mian — H5

SNACKS & STREET FOOD

23 Lao Shi Cong You Bing — F3
24 Yang's Dumplings — H2
25 Peng Yuan Guo Tie — E7
26 Jin Yun Shao Bing — D5
27 Yi Ren Yi Guo — H6
28 Da Hu Chun Qijiandian — I3
29 Bian Jie Dan Bing — F4
30 Xian Mo Rou Jia Mo — C4
31 Wuhan Three Delicacies Tofu Skin — H2

SWEETS

32 Luneurs Boulanger + Glacier — C6
33 Pan Yong Xing Rice Desserts — F3
34 Strictly Cookies — C5
35 MBD — D5
36 Pain Chaud — F6
37 Gelato dal Cuore — E3
38 Huangjin Shou Si Mianbao — E5

EARLY & LATE

39 Cha's — G4
40 Ding Te Le — G4
41 Fukuchan Fu Kao Jin Hua — F4

42 Jini Dapaidang — A8
43 Ajiya Yakiniku — E5
44 Nanjing Tangbao — E6
45 Hai Di Lao — E3
46 Beijing Mutton Hot Pot — E5
47 Fei Zai Man — F3

HOT POT

48 Qimin — E4
49 Wu Chu — J4
50 Wulao Health Elixir — E6
51 Holy Cow — A5
52 Zhen Xian Wei Zhu — F3
53 Halloween Hot Pot — F3

CLASSIC SHANGHAI

54 Old Jesse — D6
55 Jianguo328 — F6
56 Fu1088 — D4
57 Shang Zhi Jiao Can Shi — F4
58 Ren He Guan — F6
59 Old Style Ningbo — D5
60 Rui Fu Yuan — F5
61 Yuan Yuan — D6

CASUAL & CONTEMPORARY

62 Together — D4
63 Bird — E5
64 Wu Guan Tang — C6
65 Oriental House — D5
66 Wan Party — B5
67 Oha — E5
68 Kun Thai — B6
69 Okaeri — F6
70 Lotus Eatery — C5
71 Xime — E5

WESTERN

72 Diner — E5
73 Homeslice — G4
74 Mercato — I3
75 The Cannery — C4
76 Villa Le Bec — C6
77 Commune Social — E2
78 Raw — D3
79 Pirata — C5
80 RAC Bar — D5

SPECIAL OCCASION

81 Yu Zhi Lan — E4
82 Ultraviolet — J2
83 PHÉNIX at the PuLi — I2
84 Yong Yi Ting — I3
85 Canton Table — E4
86 Seventh Son
87 Bo Shanghai
88 Wujie

89 Fu He Hui — E4

COFFEE

90 Bitter — E5
91 SeeSaw — C5
92 Rumors — D6
93 Moon Coffee Roasters — F4
94 Uncle No Name Espresso — F5
95 Shanghailander (Coffee Bar) — E7
96 % Arabica Shanghai Roastery — I2

TEA

97 HeyTea — G6
98 Gui Pu Cha Kongjian — E7
99 Fan Ji Keting — D6
100 Wanling Tea House — E6
101 Xin Yuan — E6
102 YinXe Tea House — E7
103 InWe — F3

COCKTAILS

104 Senator Saloon — E5
105 Bar No. 3 — D6
106 Blackbird — C5
107 Avenue Joffre — E6
108 Epic — D5
109 Shake — F4
110 Magpie Cocktail Bar 2 — D6
111 Union Trading Company — E5

WINE

112 Le Verre à Vin — D5
113 Shanghailander Wine Café — E6
114 No Name — D4
115 Le Bec Boutique — C6
116 Vinism — D4

MARKETS & INGREDIENTS

117 Jinhua Ham Guy on Wulumuqi Lu — E5
118 Fuxing Zhong Lu Wet Market — F5
119 Pudong Muslim Market — J3
120 City Super — F5
121 Avocado Lady — E5

PRESENTS

122 Convenience Stores
123 Happy Clay — F5
124 Laoximen Tea Market — H4
125 Spin Ceramics — C1
126 Bee Cheng Hiang — F5

UNIVERSITY OF MICHIGAN

3 9015 10031 1151